Encounters
AT THE WELL

A Journey to Joy and Freedom

Encounters at the Well: A Journey to Joy and Freedom
© 2024 by Arlyn Lawrence

All rights reserved. No part of this publication may be reproduced, stored in a retrieval system, or transmitted in any form by any means—electronic, mechanical, photocopy, recording, or otherwise—except for brief quotations in critical reviews or articles, without the prior permission of the publisher, except as provided by U.S. copyright law.

Unless otherwise indicated, Scripture quotations and words of Jesus are taken or adapted from the New American Standard Bible,® Copyright © 1960, 1962, 1963, 1968, 1971, 1973, 1975, 1977, 1995 by The Lockman Foundation. Used by permission.

Scripture quotations marked (NLT) are taken from the *Holy Bible*, New Living Translation, copyright ©1996, 2004, 2015 by Tyndale House Foundation. Used by permission of Tyndale House Publishers, Carol Stream, Illinois 60188. All rights reserved.

For bulk orders and quantity discounts, email:
info@inspiralit.com

ISBN: 978-1-952943-34-8

Published by Inspira, LLC
5790 Soundview Dr., Ste. 201F, Gig Harbor, WA 98335
Book Design: PerfecType, Nashville, TN
Cover Design: Marc Whitaker

"In *Encounters at the Well*, Arlyn Lawrence lays out simple, God-directed processes for experiencing the abundant and 'infinitely more than' kind of life God designed for you."

Mike Riches, D.Min.
Pastor; Founder, The Sycamore Commission
Author of *Living Free: Recovering God's Design for Your Life* and the *Living Set Free in Christ Course*

"Arlyn has read the mail of every woman on the planet! She leaves no stone unturned in this powerful devotional study that not only speaks to the reality of how women and their relationships can go sideways, but she gives practical steps of action to be able to apply in daily life and overcome. This is a book that can be a dynamic tool in the hands of every willing woman, in order to live in the abundant life that Jesus wants to give. I want to share it with everyone I know."

Karen Crowe
Director of Healing Prayer Ministries
The Sycamore Commission, Gig Harbor, WA

"*Encounters at the Well* invites women to both know and be deeply known by Jesus. Arlyn Lawrence provides us with that rare combination of relevant biblical truth and a reality-based strategy for spiritual, emotional, and interpersonal transformation. Women will appreciate the honest and gentle way that she reveals potential blocks to the living water offered by Christ to deeply satisfy our souls."

Cindi J. Martin, LCSW
Professional Psychotherapist and
Author of *Choosing Intimacy: Exploring Christ's Model for Mutuality and Deeper Relationships*

"*Spectacular!* The word leapt from my soul at the last page of Arlyn Lawrence's book, *Encounters at the Well*. Jesus is poised to heal, but sometimes we feel too fragile, wounded, and broken to surrender ourselves to Him. In a fresh, simple way, complete with an abundance of biblical references, Arlyn imparts powerful spiritual principles for finding freedom from the things that bind us. This book will truly lead you on a journey of joy!"

Grace Running-Nichols
Author of *The Color of God*

"Challenging—yet inviting and encouraging—*Encounters at the Well* is easily accessible by people from all backgrounds, wherever they are on their faith journey. Here, profound biblical truths are made clear, understandable, and applicable, while helpfully advocating the imperative for Christians to deepen their faith in the context of living, accountable relationships.

I have known Arlyn Lawrence for many years to be a woman of great love, integrity, faith, and practical wisdom. Although her book is primarily intended for women, as a husband, father, pastor, and doctor, I found it to be both enjoyable and insightful as it stimulated and enriched my understanding and experience of God's love."

Rev. Dr. Tim Peppiatt
Anglican Priest, Family Doctor
United Kingdom

"*Encounters at the Well* invites women to look at core heart issues, bring them to Jesus, and replace them with freeing truths. It will give women's groups ways to go below the surface and talk about hurts many have experienced but have not had a space to talk about. *Encounters at the Well* will open the way to a path of freedom for many."

Connie Willems
Spiritual Director and Co-Author of *Come Talk with Me: Developing the Skill of Communicating with God*

"Arlyn Lawrence is my friend, and my editor, but I am not writing this endorsement because of either of these things. I am writing this endorsement for you, the reader! After reading *Encounters at the Well: A Journey to Joy and Freedom*, I am already planning on gathering some women together and teaching it. It is filled with truth, wisdom, and good practices for women who love Jesus."

Dawn Morris
Author of *Fire and Flood*, *One Will Be Taken*,
and *One Will Be Left*

"Arlyn Lawrence encourages women, through her book, to discover and use the potential that has been placed in them, and to overcome the obstacles of heart and soul that would hold them back. It is the condition of the heart that determines whether the value, gifts, and abilities that God has placed in individual women (and men) really come to fruition. According to Genesis 1:27, God created man in His image and likeness as male *and* female. It would be a huge loss for the Body of Christ if both were not empowered to fully exercise their God-given potential and personality. "

Dr. Martin Stoessel / Rachel Stoessel
Field Director / Marketing and Communications
Agape International, Cru Switzerland

"*Encounters at the Well*, by Arlyn Lawrence, is one of the best 'how-to' books for every seeker of God. If you deeply desire the transformation that God is calling you to, this is the book that will lead the way, guide your heart, be the light for each step for your soul. Instead of taking the stairs on your spiritual journey, Arlyn's insightful, inspired work is an escalator that will carry your soul into deeper intimacy and union with the Scriptures and God Himself."

Angela Connelly
Author of *The Crowded Table: The Brave and Beautiful Choice to Mother Many*, and *The Crowded Table 2: The Father's Voice*

"*Encounters at the Well* will take you on a deep dive into the depths of God's goodness and love. Each chapter brings truth and encouragement as you learn practical tips to go deeper in your relationship with Jesus. You will be refreshed, restored, and grounded on the promises of Jesus Christ and experience the abundant life He brings. I highly recommend!"

Katie Robertson
Executive Director, The Anchor Gathering
Author of *Live Anchored, Jesus, Our Anchor,* and
*Anchored: Walking by Faith, Living in Hope,
Remembering Karina*

So He came to a city of Samaria called Sychar, near the parcel of ground that Jacob gave to his son Joseph; and Jacob's well was there. So Jesus, being wearied from His journey, was sitting thus by the well. It was about the sixth hour.

There came a woman of Samaria to draw water. Jesus said to her, "Give Me a drink." For His disciples had gone away into the city to buy food.

The Samaritan woman said to Him, "How is it that You, being a Jew, ask me for a drink since I am a Samaritan woman?" (For Jews have no dealings with Samaritans.)

Jesus answered and said to her, "If you knew the gift of God, and who it is who says to you, 'Give Me a drink,' you would have asked Him, and He would have given you living water."

She said to Him, "Sir, You have nothing to draw with and the well is deep; where then do You get that living water? You are not greater than our father Jacob, are You, who gave us the well, and drank of it himself and his sons and his cattle?"

Jesus answered and said to her, "Everyone who drinks of this water will thirst again; but whoever drinks of the water that I will give her shall never thirst; but the water that I will give her will become in her a well of water springing up to eternal life."

John 4:5–14

CONTENTS

Foreword xi
Introduction 1

CHAPTER ONE   Meeting Jesus 3
CHAPTER TWO   Free at Last 11
CHAPTER THREE Accepted 23
CHAPTER FOUR   A Good Friend 31
CHAPTER FIVE   Forgiven 45
CHAPTER SIX   Cherished 53
CHAPTER SEVEN Secure 67
CHAPTER EIGHT Faithful 79
CHAPTER NINE   A Blessing 91

Endnotes 101
About the Author 103
Acknowledgments 105

FOREWORD

What you are about to read in this book from my dear friend, Arlyn Lawrence, is sure to awaken your heart and infuse you with life—the "rivers of living water" Jesus promised in His encounter with the woman at the well in John 4. I see that kind of life in Arlyn herself, and you will find it here in her book, as well.

I first met Arlyn at a National Prayer Committee meeting in Palm Springs, California, in 2005. When the leader asked us to take the hand of the person beside us and pray, I didn't realize that this "chance" meeting with Arlyn would change my life.

At the time, Arlyn was a contributing editor and writer for *Pray!* magazine (NavPress). A devoted wife and mother of five, she was also a trusted leader in her church and on her way to being a nationally recognized prayer and children's ministry leader. She was also an experienced leader with The Sycamore Commission, an international, transformational discipleship training that works with churches, church leaders, and individuals to bring about the restoration of the power and ministry of Jesus.

I had just written my first book, *The Prayer Saturated Church* (NavPress/Tyndale), and was working with pastors and leaders around the nation in helping to formalize and organize effective prayer ministries in their churches. Like Arlyn, I was a young woman in leadership, who had a passion for writing and teaching people to pray and walk in victory. We had a lot in common. We hit it off right away.

FOREWORD

Over the next couple of years, we found ourselves "coincidentally" running into each other at meetings across the country. It became increasingly clear that the Lord had caused our paths to intersect for some divine purpose. It wasn't long before I asked Arlyn to co-write a book with me, *Prayer-Saturated Kids: Equipping and Empowering Children in Prayer* (NavPress/Tyndale), and we began ministering together. It is rare now that a year goes by that we are not working together from a hotel room, her home, or mine, on another God project together. Arlyn has enriched my life. She has come alongside me with her gifts and talents and helped me accomplish goals I could never have done without her investment.

One of the things I love most about Arlyn is that she is deeply spiritual in a most down-to-earth sort of way. Seeing people delivered from bondage and walking in freedom is as natural for her as breathing in and out. She always has a fresh story to tell of how she has led someone to Christ or how she has prayed and seen a friend or acquaintance supernaturally healed or delivered from fear, anxiety, insecurity, or depression.

We all want to experience the freedom we know is ours through Christ Jesus. But for many of us, the way to freedom seems confusing and intimidating, even a bit scary. You will not find that to be the case as you experience this devotional. It is filled with the love of the Father. You will hear His gentle voice calling you to let go of the old ways—cycles of fear, abandonment, intimidation, bitterness, and other destructive patterns. Through the pages of this book, you will learn to walk and live in a fresh new way—one that leads to life and life more abundantly.

In our world today, we find ourselves in an unbelievable *kairos* moment in history. Like Esther, we have been born for "such a time as this." It is imperative that, as Christian women, we be walking in our authority, in freedom from all the ways the enemy has sought to oppose us, crush us, sideline us, and prevent us from fulfilling our destinies.

In this book, Arlyn will help you step into this place of hope and restoration, strength and Holy Spirit power. She will take you on a devotional experience led by the Teacher Himself, Holy Spirit. As you walk with Him through these pages, allow Him to take you into new places of intimacy and communion with your Father. It's a journey worth taking.

Cheryl Sacks
Co-Founder and Leader, BridgeBuilders International
Author of *The Prayer Saturated Church* and *Fire on the Family Altar: Experience the Holy Spirit's Power in Your Home*

INTRODUCTION

One of the (many) remarkable things about Jesus is this: *He never left anything the way He found it.* Whether it was water to wine, or a broken heart made whole, Jesus was in the transformation business from start to finish—and He is still at it today.

God's plan and purpose for each of us is to transform us into His original and beautiful design and destiny. "I came that they might have life," Jesus said, "and might have it abundantly" (John 10:10). This means us! We, too, have access to that "abundant life" through Jesus!

Through your own encounters with Jesus, through your times in His Word and His presence, and maybe even through the pages of this book, I pray God's love and grace will come alive to you in a fresh way. May His Spirit be poured out on you and His power be released in you in ever-increasing ways.

I want to point out some elements in this devotional that will greatly contribute to your getting the most out of it. I strongly encourage you to embrace them and set your heart and mind to actually speaking them aloud and doing them. It's not enough to just read them and give a mental assent. These are:

1. The 4Rs: This prayer model utilizes the biblical principles of **repenting** of sin, **rebuking** the enemy from your life, **receiving** God's forgiveness, and **replacing** the area of brokenness or sin with God's truth and your own actions of obedience. (I learned this prayer model early in my adult life from my pastor, Mike Riches, who later incorporated it into his book and course, *Living Set Free* *in Christ.* Regularly using and applying it has been life-changing for me!)

2. Declarations: These are your declarations of how you will walk, from this point on, in God's truth and in your identity as a new creation in Christ (2 Corinthians 5:17).

3. Questions for Reflection and Discussion: At the end of each chapter, there are two sections, "Heart Check" and "A Circle of Sisters." The first section, "Heart Check," is for your own personal reflection and prayer. I will warn you up front: these exercises can be hard-hitting. That being said, they should not bring condemnation as we consider ways we may be operating out of alignment with God's Word and ways. Remember: the loving, gentle voice of the Holy Spirit does not bring condemnation; it brings *conviction*. Conviction leads to repentance, which leads to freedom!

The second section, "A Circle of Sisters," can be used with a small group or prayer partner. Whether you are using this devotional on your own, with a friend, or as part of a larger group study, you indeed are part of a "circle of sisters" across time and space, women who have longed for—and have experienced—their own encounters with the Lord. Use these sections to stimulate your thinking, prayers, and actions steps as you interact with your heavenly Father and others about the themes in this book.

As you learn to use the tools of restoration and transformation God has given you through Jesus, I pray that your heart will be renewed and transformed—and that you increasingly experience the life of joy and freedom He intended you to live!

Arlyn Lawrence

CHAPTER ONE

Meeting Jesus

In John chapter 4, we meet a remarkable Samaritan woman who encountered Jesus at a well near the village of Sychar in Samaria, as He and His disciples were journeying homeward toward Galilee. We don't know her name when we first meet her; Scripture doesn't tell us that. However, Eastern Orthodox church tradition does provide some insight, telling us more of her story after she met Jesus. The disciples later gave her the name Photini, which means "enlightened one."

> *"If anyone is in Christ, they are a new creation,
> old things have passed away, and all things are made new."*
> *(2 Corinthians 5:17)*

After all, a new creation deserves a new name, right!? Here's an interesting thought: the word "new" in the verse above doesn't just mean "new" like we might get a "new car" (that is, not necessarily brand-new, but new to us). This word "new," in the original Greek language, means "prototype," i.e., "never before seen." That's because, when we put our faith in Jesus, our spirit is regenerated; we are "made alive in Christ." *We become a never-before-seen

---

*(For more on what happens spiritually when we receive Jesus into our life, read Ephesians 2:1–10 in your Bible).

creation: a human who can live two-dimensionally, "seated with him in the heavenly realms because we are united with Christ Jesus" (Ephesians 2:6, NLT).

Wow. We are seated at Christ's right hand, sharing in His identity, authority, and power, while our two feet are still physically planted on *terra firma*. We live in two dimensions, two realms, with power and authority and the very mind and presence of Christ in us. That is an amazing "new creation," don't you think?

And that's exactly what happened to Photini, in her encounter with Jesus at the well. She became a new creation. Church tradition tells us the exploits of Photini, as she apparently went on to become a major figure in the early Church and a powerful force for the gospel in the known world at that time. It is believed she even led the Roman emperor Nero's daughter and her court of servants to faith in Christ!

As we take time to consider the story of the woman at the well, and other stories in Scripture of people who had personal encounters with Jesus, **be thinking about how the same things they learned and experienced can be applied to your own life and relationship with Him.** They're not just stories. We're supposed to learn and apply the principles and lessons these stories teach us!

Take a few minutes and read the story of the woman at the well in its entirety. You'll find it in John 4:1–43.

Note how Jesus took notice of her and conversed with her, despite the cultural taboos that frowned on Jewish men speaking to women (in this case, an "unclean" Samaritan woman at that), and particularly despite the taboos on discussing personal, spiritual, or theological matters with them. Women in those days were seen, not heard, and rarely educated. Jesus blew past those barriers and went straight to the heart of the matter and the person. I believe He stands ready to do the same with each and every one of us, if we are open to Him.

The other thing I can't help but notice is how matter-of-factly Jesus spoke to Photini about her sin. He didn't shame her or moralize over her failings and shortcomings. He did, however, point out that she had made practical life choices that violated God's commandments, resulting in much heartache and sorrow and a string of broken relationships.

Photini, to her credit, didn't try to justify her situation or make excuses for her sin. Though I imagine she was startled by His forthrightness (and His accuracy), she swallowed hard and simply responded, "Sir, I perceive you are a prophet." She owned it. She repented, turned from her sin, and lived the rest of her life in the grace, mercy, and service of her loving heavenly Father.

This account in John 4 shows us that Jesus has the ability, as the Word of God Himself, to go deep into our very souls. The writer to the Hebrews wrote: "For the word of God is living and active, and sharper than any two-edged sword, even penetrating as far as the division of soul and spirit, of both joints and marrow, and able to judge the thoughts and intentions of the heart" (Hebrews 4:12). This quality of God is what prompted David to say to Him, "Search me, God, and know my heart . . . see if there is any hurtful way in me, and lead me in the everlasting way" (Psalm 139:23–24).

This is what Photini experienced when she encountered Jesus, right in the middle of a regular work day. He seeks to meet us in similar settings—maybe even in the middle of our household chores, like He did with her! That's why below, and in each chapter of this book, you'll find an opportunity for a "Heart Check" with Jesus. We can ask Him to help us search our own heart, like He did with David and Photini, and seek out the living, cleansing, liberating water He promises.

In some of the "Heart Check" sections of this study, you may, like Photini, be startled at first how matter-of-factly we are going to consider ways we may have violated God's commandments. This is not intended to inflict judgment or shame. Rather, it's to bring those things into the light of God's truth and love, like Jesus did with Photini, so we, too, can experience the refreshment and freedom that comes from repentance. "Repent, therefore," we read in Acts 3:19, "that times of refreshing may come from the presence of the Lord."

Then, remember this: after her encounter with Jesus, Photini didn't just go back to business as usual, nor did she keep her newfound freedom to herself. She shouted it from the proverbial rooftops! So here, in this devotional study, we're going to do the same. When you see opportunities to apply God's truths to your own life, apply them. When the Holy Spirit makes you aware, in your heart, of ways you've sinned against God, take advantage of the grace and forgiveness He freely offers you, and repent of them. When you see suggested declarations you can use to proclaim your newfound freedom and obedience, declare them.

Like it was for Photini, joy and freedom can be yours in Jesus.

Heart Check

I pray that out of His glorious riches He may strengthen you with power through His Spirit in your inner being, so that Christ may dwell in your hearts through faith. And I pray that you, being rooted and established in love, may have power, together with all the saints, to grasp how wide and long and high and deep is the love of Christ, and to know this love that surpasses knowledge—that you may be filled to the measure of all the fullness of God. (Ephesians 3:16–19)

Take some time alone with God. Read through Isaiah 61 in your Bible, and read it out loud, personalizing it for yourself. Instead of words like "the brokenhearted," "they," or "my people," insert your own name. Do the same with the Ephesians 3 passage above, asking Jesus to help you grasp how wide and long and high and deep His love for you is.

Then, in the space provided below, prayerfully write out a list identifying some of the ways you have been brokenhearted, wounded, disappointed, rejected, or betrayed. Can you identify any areas of emotional or spiritual captivity from which you long to be freed? How about wounds and weaknesses (emotional or physical) that need healing?

It is God's heart to give you beauty instead of ashes, the oil of gladness instead of mourning, and a garment of praise instead of a spirit of despair. He calls you an "oak of righteousness, a planting of the Lord for the display of His splendor" (Isaiah 61:3)!

A Circle of Sisters

Answer the following questions and, if you are doing this with a partner or group, share your answers with them:

1. Were there any new thoughts for you in this reading about Jesus: His love for you, or what it means to encounter Him and have Him in your life, and have Him speak to you so directly and personally? What were your impressions?

2. If you were to physically encounter Jesus, like "Photini" did at the well in John 4, what do you imagine He would say to you if He read your heart like He did hers?

3. Do you think it's true that, even if we've known Jesus and have had Him in our lives, we can get so busy, or so focused on "doing" for others, that we fail to hear His voice or receive His personal ministry toward us? If so, what does that look like, in your experience?

4. Close off with prayer for one another (or yourself, if you're doing this on your own), for eyes to see, ears to hear, and a heart to receive the love of Jesus for you as you encounter Him in newer and deeper ways in the days ahead.

ENCOUNTERS AT THE WELL

Notes and Prayers

CHAPTER TWO
Free at Last

"Freedom" can mean different things to us at different times in our lives. When we initially come to faith in Jesus, passing from a state of unbelief to belief (just like Photini at the well in John 4), that is our first taste of freedom. But even afterwards, like layers of the onion peeled off one by one, we can experience different levels of freedom from the things that weigh us down and hold us back. The more we get to know Jesus, and the more we experience His love, truth, and work in our lives, the freer we can become.

John 3:16–17
For God so loved the world that He gave His one and only Son, that whoever believes in Him shall not perish but have eternal life. For God did not send His Son into the world to condemn the world, but to save the world through Him.

Galatians 3:22
But the Scripture declares that the whole world is a prisoner of sin, so that what was promised, being given through faith in Jesus Christ, might be given to those who believe.

Jesus' ministry of restoration had two distinct components. Looking at the two verses on the previous page, can you identify the first one? (answers on page 21)

Component #1 _____

Romans 6:6–7
For we know that our old self was crucified with Him so that the body of sin might be done away with, that we should no longer be slaves to sin—because anyone who has died has been freed from sin.

Galatians 5:1
It is for freedom that Christ has set us free. Stand firm, then, and do not let yourselves be burdened again by a yoke of slavery.

Looking at the above two verses, what was the second component of Jesus' ministry of freedom?

Component #2 _____

With these Scripture passages in mind, who needs "freedom"?

_____

Did you answer, "Everyone," or, "Me!"? We *all* need freedom, every single one of us!

Question: have *you* been set free, personally, and entered into a personal relationship with Jesus by faith? If not, why not? You can pray to receive freedom right now! You simply need to:

1. Recognize you are a slave to sin, separated from God and unable to save yourself.

2. Confess this to God, and ask for His forgiveness.

3. Believe that Jesus' death on the cross and His resurrection from the dead paid the penalty incurred by your sin, and secured eternal life and freedom for you.

4. Receive God's forgiveness and freedom through Jesus in faith. It is free for the asking!

> *The jailer called for lights, rushed in and fell trembling before Paul and Silas. He then brought them out and asked, "Sirs, what must I do to be saved?" They replied,* ***"Believe in the Lord Jesus, and you will be saved—you and your household."*** *Then they spoke the word of the Lord to him and to all the others in his house. At that hour of the night the jailer took them and washed their wounds; then immediately he and all his household were baptized The jailer brought them into his house and set a meal before them; he was filled with joy because he had come to believe in God— he and his whole household. (Acts 16:29–34)*

Finding Freedom

As anyone who has known Jesus for any length of time knows, we can still experience sin and brokenness in our lives after we come to know Him. So, if faith in Jesus "sets us free," why do sincere believers who love God continue to struggle with sins: bitter or lustful thoughts, pride, depression, fear, anger, and other debilitating attitudes and behaviors? Can we be held captive to sin in a way that is not instantly resolved when we are saved? Unfortunately, yes.

Read 2 Corinthians 10:3–5. What is one way that Christians—followers of Jesus—can be held in bondage by sin and Satan?

Did you catch the word "stronghold" in this passage, in verse 4? (It may be a slightly different term in your Bible, depending on the translation you read; for example, the NASB uses the word "fortresses.") *Webster's Dictionary* describes a "stronghold" as "a fortified place; a place of security; a center or place where any particular group exerts a dominating influence."

Strongholds begin as "footholds," behaviors and deceptions that we allow to remain in our minds and hearts, and which can become a base of operations for the enemy to set up a control operation: "In your anger do not sin: Do not let the sun go down while you are still angry, and do not give the devil a foothold" (Ephesians 4:26–27). Left unchecked, these footholds evolve into deeply ingrained habits, wrong thoughts, and belief systems that "set themselves up against the knowledge of God" (2 Corinthians 10:5). These belief systems and behaviors can eventually begin to exert a dominating influence in our life and personality and can be an "open door," so to speak, to the enemy (i.e., the devil) in our life.

Often we recognize the symptoms of a stronghold, but have suppressed the circumstances that provided the original footing it is built on. This can leave us feeling helpless and hopeless, wondering why we are unable to control certain attitudes and behaviors. We may be completely blind to the symptoms of our strongholds, and need others to speak truth into our lives to make us aware of them.

Examples of Strongholds

- anger, rage, hatred
- insecurity
- pride, religious pride
- fear
- hopelessness
- inferiority
- selfish ambition
- addiction
- jealousy
- betrayal
- self-centeredness
- vanity, conceit
- apathy, passivity
- bitterness
- self-pity
- critical spirit
- self-hatred
- covetousness, envy
- perfectionism
- striving
- insignificance

This is not a comprehensive list of the ways wrong thinking can dominate our perceptions, worldview, thinking, and behavior, but it gives an idea of the kinds of issues that can operate as "stronghold" issues in our lives. If you think any of these might have a hold on you, it doesn't have to stay that way. Jesus came to set us free from *everything* that keeps us down and holds us back. Everything means . . . *everything!*

You *can* break the chains of strongholds and sin patterns from your heart and life. Use these guidelines below—the 4 Rs[1]—as you pray through the areas of heart restoration you'll find in this prayer journey:

1. Repent of the sin. Call it what it is. It may be a heart attitude, like bitterness, rebellion, or pride. It could be a behavior, like alcohol abuse, immorality, or stealing. It could even be a feeling, like rejection, inferiority, or shame, which you allow to mark you and even to become part of your identity.

    "Repent, then, and turn to God, so that your sins may be wiped out, that times of refreshing may come from the Lord." (Acts 3:19)

2. Rebuke the enemy and resist his hold on you because of it, through the power of Jesus' death and resurrection.

    "Jesus said to him, 'Away from me, Satan!'" (Matthew 4:10)

    "Submit yourselves, then, to God. Resist the devil, and he will flee from you." (James 4:7)

3. <u>Replace</u> the old attitudes, actions, and emotions with ones that are consistent with the heart and character of Jesus Christ, and the truth of God's Word.

"You were taught, with regard to your former way of life, to put off your old self, which is being corrupted by its deceitful desires; to be made new in the attitude of your minds; and to put on the new self, created to be like God in true righteousness and holiness." (Ephesians 4:22–24)

4. <u>Receive</u> God's forgiveness and cleansing. Ask Him to fill you anew with His Holy Spirit to strengthen you to think, behave, and feel rightly.

"If we confess our sins, He is faithful and just and will forgive us our sins and purify us from all unrighteousness." (1 John 1:9)

Heart Check

Jesus had a profound love for individual people, and a deep desire to see them live in wholeness—spiritually, emotionally, and physically. His utmost desire was to see people freed from the bondage of sin and restored to their heavenly Father. Jesus was not discriminating in His compassion. He loved men, women, and children. He esteemed the rich and the poor alike. He had a special regard for the outcast, the shamed, the broken, and the infirm.

Jesus demonstrated what God's heart for His people looked like as He healed the sick, transformed the brokenhearted, cast out demons, and gave life and hope to those who thought they had lost it. Besides the woman at the well (John 4), there was Zacchaeus (Luke 19:2–10), and the woman Jesus healed from an issue of blood (Matthew 9:20–22). These are only three of many whose broken lives and hearts were made whole by the love and ministry of Jesus.

Take a moment now and look up and read these stories before we go on to consider what an encounter with Jesus might look like in our own lives. What stands out to you about these people's interactions with Jesus?

What are some things they had in common?

What did they receive from Him?

Do you see any similarities between their own lives and concerns, and your own?

Write any other observations below.

A Circle of Sisters

Answer the following questions and share your responses with your small group:

1. Consider this statement on page 11: *"If faith in Jesus 'sets us free,' why do sincere believers who love God continue to struggle with sin?"* After this lesson, what is your answer to this question?

2. What would you hope to receive from Jesus if you had a face-to-face encounter with Him, the way Photini—the woman at the well—did in John 4? Does your answer to this question reveal any areas of your life, heart, or thinking that need Jesus' touch and freedom?

3. Take some time to pray for one another about these things in each others' lives. If you are comfortable, you can use the 4-R outline on page 14, either on your own or with a group if you're in one—repent, rebuke, replace, receive. This is not a formula, but it is a helpful model to guide your conversation with God as you seek freedom from these areas.

*Here's a sample prayer outline: "Lord, I **repent** for my sin of (blank), and **rebuke** the enemy and his influence in my life because of it. I will **replace** (name the sin) with walking in the opposite action or attitude (name it). I **receive** Your forgiveness, Lord, and Your Holy Spirit. Fill me and help me walk in alignment with Your love and truth."*

Answers to questions on page 12:

1. to free people from the ETERNAL prison of sin and death
2. to free people from IMMEDIATE captivity to bondages, infirmities, and sins
3. EVERYONE!

ENCOUNTERS AT THE WELL

Notes and Prayers

CHAPTER THREE

accepted

*The Lord your God is in your midst, a victorious warrior.
He will exult over you with joy, He will be quiet in His love,
He will rejoice over you with shouts of joy.
(Zephaniah 3:17)*

When people are colorblind, they don't know what other people see. They just know what *they* see. Just for fun, look up on YouTube a video of someone who has put on, for the first time, a pair of color correction lenses designed to help colorblind people see the world more realistically. The responses are heartwarming! The world takes on a whole new appearance when the lenses through which they view life are corrected.

Like colorblindness or a pair of tinted sunglasses, certain strongholds rooted in strong emotions can be lenses that dramatically alter the way we see life. They affect the way our brain and our emotions receive, interpret, and process the sensory and relational stimuli that come at us on a daily basis. *Rejection* is like that.

From scientists to sociologists, all research confirms that it is a fundamental need of every human being to be born into love, and to be loved and accepted. God's original design was for people to grow up in an environment of love, warmth, unconditional acceptance, and adoration. But for many of us, this doesn't happen. Some, from the very start of their lives, grow up with various degrees of brokenness, rejection, and abandonment.

Some people—and perhaps this includes you—grow up believing they are a nuisance, never receiving the fullness of the love and affirmation and security and celebration that was intended for them by God's design. This becomes their "normal" and, from a very young age, they begin to learn to cope with it. Their identity never becomes who it was designed to be; their very personhood is crippled.

Rejection doesn't need to be a lifelong pattern in order to affect us deeply. Divorce, or the loss of a long-term relationship or friendship, can embed roots of rejection in us. A significant job loss, any kind of prejudice or racism, experiencing poverty or a "less-than" mentality, and other situations can leave us feeling rejected to the point it becomes the lens through which we see the world.

If this process is not interrupted, we can experience and see the world *through a lens of rejection*. Eventually, we may even pass on to others the same lack of affection/love/acceptance they have experienced, and the cycle of rejection continues.

Read the following passages and note what they tell you about God's love for you:

Psalm 139: 13–18

Jeremiah 1: 4–7

These messages were not just for Old Testament times. They were recorded for you and me as an assurance and constant reminder that we all were formed, loved, and planned for in the mind and heart of God the Father, before we ever entered this world and took our first breath. Regardless of our life circumstances or how other humans have regarded or treated us, we are loved. We are wanted. We are valued.

YOU are loved. YOU are wanted. YOU are valued.

Where the lie comes in is different for each of us. Rejection can enter our lives in various ways. Sometimes it is "inherited," because our parents themselves lived under rejection. People who have been rejected end up rejecting others, even (and especially) those closest to them. What might that look like? See the list below and ask the Lord to highlight any that apply to you.

Heart Check

Do you struggle with rejection? Here are some symptoms to help you self-assess. Prayerfully go through them and check all that apply to you (even if only a little bit).

- ❏ I find it difficult to freely accept or give demonstrations of love and affection.
- ❏ I don't believe people when I am paid a compliment.
- ❏ I never feel fully a part of things; I always feel like I'm on the outside of the "circle," even if there isn't one.
- ❏ I am performance-oriented.
- ❏ I need to be needed, so I continually place myself in situations where I feel others cannot do without my help, my presence, my abilities, my ministry, etc.
- ❏ I have a low image of my appearance, my abilities, and my adequacy to succeed.
- ❏ I often buy too much—acquiring possessions/shopping validates me and makes me feel better.
- ❏ I try to make friends with important people; this makes me feel accepted and important.
- ❏ I tend to be demanding of my friends/spouse/family members because I don't feel valuable. If they don't meet up to my expectations, I become angry with them and may reject them. (This creates a cycle of heavy expectations, neediness, and rejection and broken relationships.)
- ❏ I am possessive in relationships.
- ❏ When confronted about something I may have done wrong, my immediate reaction is defensiveness and even defiance.
- ❏ I am inhibited in honestly sharing my deepest feelings with others, even with those close to me.
- ❏ I put up barriers/boundaries in my relationships because I can't let people come to close; when they do, I abort the relationship before they have the chance to really hurt me.
- ❏ I have created and strive to maintain a social media presence (Instagram, Facebook, etc.) that convinces others I am

someone I'm not, or portrays who I *want* to be, not necessarily who I really am.
❏ I live in other people's heads, imagining what they must be thinking of me.
❏ I have tended to look for love in sexual relationships, accepting or confusing sex with real intimacy to get the real love I long for.
❏ I use—and may even be addicted to—drugs and/or alcohol to falsely comfort my sense of rejection with the sense of well-being or euphoria they provide.

The temptation for any of us, when we are faced with the fear of rejection (either real or perceived), is to resort to the coping mechanisms on which we have depended for most, if not all, of our lives. These coping mechanisms are anything we have learned to do or use in order to comfort ourselves in the face of rejection. These coping mechanisms are essentially "false comforts," because they may make us feel a little better temporarily, but don't solve the root problem. Like a placebo, they trick us into thinking we've alleviated the symptoms of our pain, but they really do nothing to heal us.

To what extent are you viewing life and relationships through a lens of rejection? Go back to the checklist above and see how many and which boxes you checked. Using the 4-R prayer model you've learned, take these things to your heavenly Father in prayer. Talk to Him about them:

1. **Repenting** of any and all attitudes and actions associated with *rejection.*
2. **Rebuking** and renouncing the lies and influence of the enemy in your life because of them.

3. **Replacing** the lies with truth, confidence, and *security in God's love for you,* by continually renewing your mind in His Word and in His Spirit.
4. **Receiving** His forgiveness, and being filled by His Holy Spirit. God's Spirit in you will help you live in the truth of His love for you. Seek Him—the Holy Spirit—and depend on Him at all times (no false comforts!) to walk free of rejection.

Look up Romans 8: 31–39. What does this passage tell you about God's love for you, and what that means for you? Use the space below to write a note to God, thanking Him for His love, and telling Him what living in that love is going to look like for you from now on.

A Circle of Sisters

This chapter may be difficult for some women in whom the stronghold of rejection and its lies run deeply in their thinking and even their personalities. As friends and sisters in Christ, this is an opportunity to support and affirm one another in your identities in light of God's great love and acceptance.

Make a list of five qualities you believe are important or meaningful about yourself—such as a gift or talent (e.g., musical, artistic, a good leader, athletics/fitness, a great cook, etc.), things that make you a good friend/mom/wife/daughter/employee, etc. (e.g., loyal, a good listener), a good partner (e.g., supportive, emotionally available), or a good teammate/co-worker (e.g., responsible, strong work ethic). Thank the Lord for making you this way!

If time and opportunity allow, pray for one another and ask God to show you aspects of His original design for each of you. Share with each other what God brings to your mind about that person as you pray for them. (e.g., "Karen is generous, full of compassion, and always ready with a word of encouragement for others.") This can be a wonderful encouragement!

Then, make the following declarations (aloud, if possible), either on your own or with your prayer partner or group of friends. If you are in a group, pray for one another. Pray for God's help and grace to walk in these truths. You can do this by the power of the Holy Spirit in you, assuring you of the Father's great love for you:

- ❏ I will immerse myself in the truth of God's Word about who I really am: how much He loves me, accepts me, and demonstrates His faithfulness to me.
- ❏ I will not accept the lies of the enemy—perhaps planted into my mind and reinforced since childhood—that I am unloved, unaccepted, unworthy, and rejected.
- ❏ I will treat other people based on the truth of God's Word, not on my own fears, hurts, and insecurities: I will forgive. I will extend blessing. I will freely love and accept others.
- ❏ I will demonstrate encouragement, blessing, and affection to others.
- ❏ I will honestly express my thoughts and feelings to others without fear of rejection.
- ❏ I will no longer use rebellion (or a rebellious attitude) as a way of expressing my anger over feeling rejected.

- ❏ I will no longer try to "do" for others so they will love and accept me.
- ❏ I will not fear weakness and vulnerability with my spouse (or friends, family, etc.). I will trust God to protect my heart and support me.
- ❏ I will not be critical or resentful of those whom I feel have rejected me, or whom I feel walk in greater freedom, acceptance, or confidence than I do.
- ❏ I will not be critical towards myself; I will reject thoughts of self-accusation, self-hatred, and self-condemnation when they come my way.
- ❏ I will not seek comfort in self-pity and isolation.
- ❏ I will not choose false comforts for a spirit of rejection. I will not look for love in sexual relationships, seek to numb my pain through drugs, alcohol, or shopping, or live vicariously through an image I create on social media.
- ❏ I will initiate actions, attitudes, and words of comfort and encouragement to others, regardless of what I think they think of me or how I think they will receive it.
- ❏ I will just "be myself" and be comfortable with how God made me.
- ❏ I will share my faith in Jesus and what He's done for me with whomever, and whenever, the Holy Spirit gives me an opportunity.

Remember, God is for you—He is your biggest fan! There is nothing you need do to earn His love and favor. You are His beloved daughter and nothing can separate you from His love.

CHAPTER FOUR
a Good Friend

*Two are better than one because they have
a good return for their labor.
For if either of them falls, the one will lift up his companion.
But woe to the one who falls
when there is not another to lift him up.*
(Ecclesiastes 4:9–10)

Generally speaking, women tend to find their identity and significance in their relationships. That can make the area of friendships a significant area of vulnerability for us—and the enemy knows it! Scripture warns us that the devil is a prowling lion, looking to devour us (1 Peter 5:8). Many times, he uses our relationships to do it.

What woman has not experienced a struggle in initiating or maintaining life-giving friendships with other women? Let's be honest; which of us, over the years, has not battled with building walls of protection to protect ourselves from woundedness resulting from cattiness, backstabbing, and betrayal?

Each of us has a history: where we came from, who our families were and are, the kinds of relationships and circumstances we've experienced in life. And though, in Christ, we are all "new creations" (2 Corinthians 5:17), our past experiences still have a great deal of influence on our self-image, our worldview, and the way we interact with others. If we've lived in the world any length of time, not many of us have avoided wounding in this area. It's an unfortunate yet common part of the human experience. Because of it, it is very likely that, over the years, we have built up strongholds of thinking and behaving that:

- prevent us from initiating relationships
- inhibit us from being transparent and vulnerable
- compel us to compare and compete versus bless and encourage
- cause us to isolate and/or keep our circle small, safe, or comfortable

Do you ever feel, when it comes to your relationships with other women:

- unnoticed in the crowd?
- unsure of your significance?
- driven to compete or perform?
- compelled to jockey for position?
- forced to withdraw to protect yourself?

If so, then read on—and be encouraged and hopeful! Just as Jesus came to bring restoration to every place in our lives that has been broken, He came to redeem this one.

Healing Our Hearts in the Area of Friendship

We all have the desire to be affirmed and accepted by a circle of friends. For some women, the desired circle is large, with many relationships and activities. Other women are content with a more intimate circle of close friends, and less interaction. But whatever our temperament and comfort level, we all need friends. We need to *have* friends. And we need to *be* a friend.

Take time to consider your friendships today. Do you have friends who sharpen you and challenge you to be who God designed you to be, who make you wiser and compel you to be better just by being around them? Are you that friend to anyone?

Before we reach out to others, we may need to do a little heart work in ourselves first. Here are some truths to remember. Look up these Scriptures passages below and spend some time meditating on them. Pray and ask God to examine your heart and expose if there is any darkness or deception there about these truths. Jot down your thoughts as you listen to the Holy Spirit in prayer. What is He speaking to you about them?

Ephesians 2:8–9

Psalm 103:8–14

Romans 8:1

1 John 1:9

When we do not have these truths securely fastened in our heart and guiding our actions and reactions, we may find ourselves compelled to strive, perform, or be anxious or fearful. These "lies" that get whispered in our ears prevent us from entering into God's rest and provision. They poison our motives and destroy our ability to enjoy relationships of any kind. These lies can make us self-focused, and inhibit us from being selfless, free-flowing vessels of God's Holy Spirit. They prevent us from experiencing God's great gift of enjoying friends and being a friend.

With that in mind, let's take a look at three issues in particular that we may be struggling with related to having strong, godly, life-giving friendships with other women. God wants to heal us of them, and set us free to experience His generous gift and blessing of friendship!

Heart Check

Go through the following lists to see how insecurity, comparison, and competition have compromised your ability to sustain meaningful, godly relationships with other women. In your prayer groups, discuss and then use the 4Rs (repent, rebuke, replace, receive) to pray through the items you checked.

1. Insecurity

Insecurity is rooted in fear, which is basically unbelief that God is who He says He is, that He will do what He says He will do, and that His love for us is real. It is a form of unbelief that causes us to think that we are not who God says we are.

Am I living in insecurity with regard to friendships?

- ❏ I am always worried about what other women are thinking of me.
- ❏ I am afraid of being myself, for fear others will reject me.
- ❏ I have been betrayed before, and I am distrustful of other women.
- ❏ I do not like to be transparent, because it makes me feel vulnerable and out of control.
- ❏ I need frequent verbal or physical affirmations/displays of friendship in order to feel significant and valued.
- ❏ I am demanding of my friends' time and attention.
- ❏ I rush into intimacy quickly in friendships, instead of waiting for them to build slowly and naturally over time.
- ❏ If too long goes between visits, conversations, or activities with my friend (s), I feel rejected and defeated.
- ❏ I put myself in positions where other people need and depend on me, because I need to feel needed in order to prove my self-worth.
- ❏ I go above and beyond what is expected of me as a friend, in order to prove my loyalty and secure the friendship.

When you tear down the strongholds of the enemy that keep you locked down in fear of rejection, you can move OUT of insecurity and INTO the security you have in Christ. Check any boxes that apply to you. Confess them to the Lord in your prayer time and ask Him for healing and freedom in these areas.

Uproot the lie of insecurity, which says:
"I am not really who God's Word says I am. I cannot really count on His unconditional acceptance, love, confidence, protection, and strength. I must constantly be on guard against rejection. I have to take my own steps to secure my emotional protection, either by withdrawing or striving."

Replace it with the truth instead:
- ❏ I believe God's promises are unfailing.
- ❏ Everything His Word says about His accepting me, loving me, rejoicing over me, protecting me, and providing for me, is true.
- ❏ How other people treat me or react to me has no bearing on who I am in Christ.
- ❏ I will not relate to my husband, family, other women, or anyone based on my own fears, inadequacies, or sense of rejection.
- ❏ I will walk filled with the Holy Spirit, and trust the Lord Jesus to be my strength, my defender, and dearest Friend.
- ❏ I will pour myself into others, instead of trying to protect or promote myself.
- ❏ I will walk securely in faith and obedience, and in His calling on my life, regardless of what I perceive others may be saying or thinking.

Jeremiah 1:5–7
"'Before I formed you in the womb I knew you, before you were born I set you apart; I appointed you as a prophet to the nations.' 'Ah, Sovereign LORD,' I said, 'I do not know how to speak; I am only a child.' But the LORD said to me, 'Do not say, "I am only a child." You must go to everyone I send you to and say whatever I command

you. Do not be afraid of them, for I am with you and will rescue you,' declares the LORD."

Zephaniah 3:17
"The LORD your God is with you, he is mighty to save. He will take great delight in you, he will quiet you with his love, he will rejoice over you with singing."

2. Comparison

Comparison is closely related to insecurity. It is the belief that my identity and value lie in my appearance and abilities, and that I have been less endowed with these than others.

Am I living with comparison?
- ❏ I look at other women and compare myself to them in dress, appearance, body, personality, home, children, marriage, etc.
- ❏ I struggle with feeling like I never measure up to other women.
- ❏ When I walk into a room, I make a mental note of what everyone is wearing and how I compare.
- ❏ I have a tendency to make choices and decisions based on what other women are doing, rather than on what God has called *me* to do.
- ❏ I think my dating life/relationship/marriage should look like that of my friends . . . and feel defeated if it doesn't.
- ❏ When I see other women's social media posts, I often feel defeated, like I don't measure up (appearance, relationships, lifestyle, possessions, etc.)

Uproot the lie of comparison, which says:
"God made a mistake when He made me. I believe that true beauty is measured by appearance and style, and I do not measure up. When He gave out abilities, I was at the end of the line, and I got short-changed. If only I could be more like her . . ."

Plant the truth instead:
- ❏ I have been intricately and purposefully created according to a marvelous blueprint.
- ❏ My beauty is found in the inner person of my heart, which shows on my countenance, and brings joy to God and others.
- ❏ God gave me the perfect abilities to complete His calling on my life: no more, no less.
- ❏ I will not give in to self-focus or self-pity; I will rejoice in God's perfect design and plan for me.
- ❏ In Christ, I am complete.

Psalm 139:13–14
"For you created my inmost being; you knit me together in my mother's womb. I praise you because I am fearfully and wonderfully made; your works are wonderful, I know that full well."

1 Corinthians 12:16–20
"And if the ear should say, 'Because I am not an eye, I do not belong to the body,' it would not for that reason cease to be part of the body. If the whole body were an eye, where would the sense of hearing be? If the whole body were an ear, where would the sense of smell be? But in fact God has arranged the parts in the body, every one of them, just as he wanted them to be. If they were all one part, where would the body be? As it is, there are many parts, but one body."

3. Competition

Competition is rooted in pride. It is seeking recognition and preeminence at others' expense. It may not only be a competition against other people, but may also be against a standard, either real or perceived. Related issues may be performance, striving, and ambition.

Do I struggle with competition?

❏ I desire intimacy with other women, but find it blocked by feelings of jealousy and resentment.
❏ When a friend confesses a weakness, I feel glad that I'm better off than she is. Other people's flaws make me feel better about my own.
❏ I have trouble freely rejoicing in the successes of other women. I wonder, *Why her?*, or, *When will it be my turn?*
❏ I boast about my other friendships, my marriage, my children, my accomplishments, etc.
❏ I want other women to admire me and want to be like me.
❏ I strive to be like certain other women, and then better.

Uproot the lie of competition, which says:
"My value and identity are found in accomplishing goals, and in being recognized and admired. I am responsible to create my own opportunities. I need to look out for myself, to secure and maintain my reputation and position. My ultimate goal is to be significant."

Plant the truth instead:
- ❏ My significance is not based on my appearance, abilities, or accomplishments.
- ❏ My value and identity are secure in God's creating me, choosing me, and using me in His capacity and timing.
- ❏ I will not live for my own ambitions any longer, nor for the admiration and appreciation of others.
- ❏ By the power of God's Holy Spirit in me, I will die to myself, as Jesus did, and live seeking the good of others before my own.
- ❏ My ultimate goal is to give my life away in helping other women be reconciled to their Savior, and to be restored to God's original design for them.
- ❏ I will serve others with joy.
- ❏ I will accept friendship and relational intimacy from other women without feeling like I need to measure up to them or be better than them.
- ❏ I will rejoice freely in other women's successes, and celebrate with them.
- ❏ I will encourage and spur my friends on to go past me. I will support them and build them up in their other relationships and endeavors.

Matthew 23:11–12
"The greatest among you will be your servant. For whoever exalts himself will be humbled, and whoever humbles himself will be exalted."

A GOOD FRIEND

Philippians 2:5–7
"Your attitude should be the same as that of Christ Jesus: Who, being in very nature God, did not consider equality with God something to be grasped, but made himself nothing, taking the very nature of a servant, being made in human likeness."

James 4:10
"Humble yourselves before the Lord, and he will lift you up."

When we identify these weeds in the fields of our hearts, we have to root them out immediately. We cannot be passive or apathetic about them. They must come out at all costs. Let's be very clear: the weeds we are talking about are not dandelions. They are insidious, highly toxic intruders that we cannot tolerate in our fields! To uproot them, you need to:

Repent of living with insecurity, comparison, and competition. (They cause us to live in constant state of striving instead of a constant state of rest.)

Rebuke the devil's influence in your life because of them.

Replace them with the truth. Cultivate the opposite attitudes and behaviors.

Receive God's love and forgiveness and the filling of His Holy Spirit. Rest in them!

A Circle of Sisters

Some things to think about and discuss:

1. How have your past relationships (family, other friends, marriage(s), etc.) contributed to and/or inhibited your ability to initiate and sustain meaningful, healthy relationships with other women?

2. Of the "lies" mentioned in this chapter that women can believe about themselves or others, which ones sounded the most familiar to you? How have you seen these play out in your or others' lives and relationships?

3. Of the "truths" mentioned in this chapter, which ones most encouraged, challenged, convicted, or inspired you? How do you plan to implement them in your thinking, attitudes, or actions?

4. On your own or with your prayer partner or group of friends, share specifically how some of the issues you checked on the lists pertain to you, and what action plan God has given you to move out of them specifically. Pray with and for one another, and encourage each other along the way!

Notes and Prayers

CHAPTER FIVE
Forgiven

*Bear with one another, and forgive each other,
whoever has a complaint against anyone;
just as the Lord forgave you, so also should you.
(Colossians 3:13)*

Water was a precious commodity in Bible times, especially in the desert. Peoples' survival depended on finding it. As it was often desperately scarce, this was not an easy task! Not surprisingly, locating, establishing, and defending a reliable water supply was an extremely important and time-consuming priority. So was defending it.

Because of their strategic importance, wells were the center of village life, as we saw in the story of Jesus and the woman at the well in John 4. They were often centers of conflict as well, water supplies being common targets of enemy attacks. To fill in a well with dirt or stones was considered an act of war.

Our spiritual wells are no less vulnerable. Sometimes we find ourselves running dry—we pour out, and pour out, and suddenly find there's nothing left. Our relationship with the Lord seems strained and lackluster. We lose our joy. We get irritable and critical. We fall far too easily into sin. The things of this world seem more real and more important than the things of God. The "water" is backed up somewhere—blocked, and we can't seem to unstop it. What's going on?

What's Blocking Your Well?

Remember that we have an enemy who seeks, at all costs, to cut off our water supply. The goal of our adversary, the devil, is to keep us separated from feeling the love of God, from experiencing the presence and power of His Holy Spirit, and from extending Jesus' ministry to others. From our earliest years, he sets out to "fill in our wells," so to speak.

Childhood hurts and abuses establish a bedrock foundation for the enemy's schemes. On top of them, one by one, he throws more stones into the wells of our hearts, some big, some small. An unkind word. A slight misunderstanding. A strained relationship. These are pebbles. They sink to the bottom, seemingly unnoticed. Over time, we continue to suffer disappointments, unmet expectations, and betrayals. Soon, unresolved hurts and misunderstandings don't sink so easily anymore. Before we realize what has happened, our spiritual wells are effectively blocked by a dam of unforgiveness and bitterness.

The apostle Paul tells us how these two issues affect us:

> *"In your anger do not sin: do not let the*
> *sun go down while you are still angry,*
> *and do not give the devil a foothold."*
> *(Ephesians 4:26–27)*

When we allow negative emotions to remain with us—whether they be anger, hurt, fear, disappointment, or any other feelings the circumstances provoke—we give the devil a "foothold." Some versions of the Bible translate this word as "opportunity." The word in the original Greek text was *topos*. This implies a tangible spot in the same way that there was no *topos* (room) for Mary and Joseph in the inn (Luke 2:7), and that Jesus has gone to prepare a *topos* (place) for us in heaven (John 12:2–3).

Even the slightest bit of a negative emotion that we nurture—*any* offense, *any* hurt, *any* resentment—grants a small (or large) place to the devil, in which he places a stone of bitterness or unforgiveness. After a while, those stones fill in our wells, and the release of God's Holy Spirit into our life is effectually blocked—cutting off our Water Supply, and inhibiting our ability to relate properly to God and the people around us—even the people we love most.

"See to it that no one misses the grace of God
and that no bitter root grows up to cause trouble and defile many."
(Hebrews 12:15)

Do you want the living water of God's Holy Spirit to flow uninhibitedly from your innermost being, as Jesus promised? Then it's time to go down into the well of your heart and start hammering at those rocks. As we have been forgiven, we too can forgive. Yes, it might feel unpleasant, maybe even downright painful. It's dark down there. It's dirty and mucky. Some of those emotional boulders are pretty heavy. But you have to get them out. As you do, you can use the truth of God's word to utterly destroy the bedrock foundation of hurts that the enemy has laid at the bottom.

"Is not my word like fire," declares the LORD,
"and like a hammer that breaks a rock in pieces?"
(Jeremiah 23:29)

Heart Check

Resolving bitterness may take some work. Make a list of the people or circumstances you feel have hurt or wronged you. Think in the present, and as far back into the past as you can. Ask the Lord to bring the memories to your mind that He wants healed.

Mother _____

Father _____

Stepmother _____

Stepfather _____

Siblings _____

Grandparents _____

Aunts, uncles, cousins _____

Childhood friends and neighbors _____

Teachers _____

Husband _____

Boyfriend/Ex-boyfriend _____

Children _____

Employers or coworkers _____

Church leaders or church family _____

Friends _____

Neighbors _____

Ask yourself, "Who is going to pay for this?" Is the answer in your head, *The other person*!? If so, then you have not yet forgiven. Forgiveness means that you will turn the responsibility for the emotional pain and consequences of another person's sin or offense over to God. In some cases, this only has to happen in your own heart. In other instances, it may involve finding deliberate, practical ways to demonstrate your forgiveness to the person who offended or hurt you, if that is appropriate.

As it was in Bible times, filling in someone else's well is an act of WAR! Remember, "our struggle is not against flesh and blood, but against the rulers, against the authorities, against the powers of this dark world and against the spiritual forces of evil in the heavenly realms" (Ephesians 6:12). Some of us have been allowing our spiritual enemy, the devil, to drop his stones into our wells for far too long. Let's get them out of there!

4 Rs for Unforgiveness

Repent of every stone of hurt, disappointment, betrayal, and anger that you have allowed to settle at the bottom of your well.

Rebuke the devil's influence in your life because of them. Renounce the comfort you have received by hanging on to them.

Replace them with the comfort of God's Holy Spirit. Release your offenders completely, with no expectation that they will ever make things right with you. Pray that God would bless them. (If they have passed away, pray for His blessing on their memory, and on the ongoing effects of their lives.)

Receive God's forgiveness, and the fresh release of His Spirit.

During a quiet time between you and the Lord, pray through your list of offenses on pages 48–49, individually surrendering each incident and name. Imagine yourself handing the pain or anger to Jesus, who is saying: "Come to me, all you who are weary and burdened, and I will give you rest" (Matthew 11:28).

A Circle of Sisters

1. There is a saying that "bitterness is like taking poison and expecting the other person to die." How do you think this is true? How does bitterness affect us?

2. Why is forgiveness so difficult sometimes?

3. Can you think of a time that you or someone you know forgave, even when it was difficult, and experienced tremendous freedom and restoration as a result? What happened? Share this experience with the group and discuss how you can see Jesus' principles of forgiveness in it.

4. Is there a specific offense, betrayal, or wound that you know you need to extend forgiveness to someone for? Either as a group, or splitting off into pairs, spend some time praying for one another and any specific situations that are shared in your circle. Together, affirm the following truths as declarations:

- ❏ I will not nurse the false comforts of self-pity and bitterness.
- ❏ I will allow the Holy Spirit, the true Comforter, to fill my mind with thoughts and scriptures of God's comfort.
- ❏ I will extend to others the mercy and forgiveness that has God has granted to me.
- ❏ Where appropriate, I will demonstrate forgiveness in practical ways to those who have wronged me.
- ❏ From this point on, I make the commitment to hold no offenses—toward my family, my husband, my church family, friends, neighbors, co-workers, or anyone else.
- ❏ I will keep short accounts in all my relationships.

Notes and Prayers

_____

_____

_____

_____

_____

_____

_____

_____

_____

CHAPTER SIX
Cherished

"No one whose hope is in you will ever be put to shame..."
(Psalm 25:3)

What little girl doesn't dream of being a princess? Whether she is five, twenty-five, or fifty, every woman, in her heart of hearts, wants to feel beautiful, and to be desired, jealously pursued, and adored.

This is exactly the kind of love that our King, our heavenly Father, has for His daughters.

He loves us.
He cherishes us.
He jealously seeks us out and protects us.

*"... as a bridegroom rejoices over his bride,
so will your God rejoice over you."*
(Isaiah 62:5)

For many women, though, this kind of love seems more of a far-off dream than it is a present reality. At some point, the enemy came into their lives with lies and deceptions to convince them that God is not this kind of Father. Many bought the lie that their God-given desire to feel beautiful, cherished, and protected could only be found in a relationship—or relationships—with men.

For some of us, the lies entered through sexual abuse. Through the sin of others inflicted on us, our concepts of love, beauty, and relationship were distorted. According to commonly quoted statistics, roughly a third of all women admit to having been sexually abused. If women who do not freely confess it are included in the numbers, it is more likely half. One in two of us. That's a lot of hurting sisters. And the all-too-common story of many is that the abuse triggered shame and self-worth issues that propelled them into any number of other related outcomes.

Dealing with Shame

The gutting feeling of shame causes us to withhold ourselves in all areas of life. Although there are a number of reasons we may experience shame's torment, here we are particularly talking about shame related to sexuality. Many Bible commentators believe that this is why Photini was drawing water from the well at that uncommon hour: in order to avoid being there at the same time as the other women in the village—because of her shame.

In shame's shadow, we tend to form shallow and guarded relationships. We fear that someone will discover our "secret," whatever that may be, real or perceived. Some of us hide. Others become determined to prove to themselves or others that they are not what they feel. But no matter how it is manifested, shame is like an unseen weight we drag through life.

The following excerpt is from Stormie Omartian's book, *Lord, I Want to Be Whole*, about her interaction with her counselor, Mary

Anne. I include it here because it is such an accurate description of what it feels like to be caught in—and to walk out of—the enemy's deceptive stronghold of shame:

> *"It's especially important to include every sexual sin you have ever committed," Mary Anne had instructed me the first time I saw her, when she asked me to go home and list my sins.*
>
> *How embarrassing, I thought. My desperate need for love, approval, and closeness had been so strong that I'd fallen into one wrong relationship after another. It would be mortifying to tell her about all that.*
>
> *"You don't have to go into any detail," Mary Anne added, as if she knew exactly what I was thinking. "Just put down the name, confess your involvement, and ask God to restore you. We'll pray over the whole list next time."*
>
> *As I left her office I immediately started remembering various instances, and each one made me cringe. I found it felt good to write it on my 'sin list,' confessing it to God and asking forgiveness just as she told me to do, like the release that comes from telling a bad secret. I had confessed it. God had forgiven it. As long as I didn't do it again, it was done. I felt cleansed and new. I discovered that sexual purity and responsibility contribute to a sense of well-being and cause a person to feel good about herself."*[2]

As long our shame remains in the dark, it is a part of the kingdom of darkness. But when we confess our sins and bring them out into the light, we break the hold Satan has over them and us. We are forgiven. We are cleansed. We are restored. *"If we confess our sins, he is faithful and just and will forgive us our sins and purify us from all unrighteousness." (1 John 1:9)*

God wants His daughters to be released from the chains of shame, and to live out our design and destiny as royal daughters in a royal kingdom. If you are a child of God, that IS your destiny—and your identity.

> *"For he has clothed me with garments of salvation*
> *and arrayed me in a robe of righteousness,*
> *as a bridegroom adorns his head like a priest,*
> *and as a bride adorns herself with her jewels."*
> *(Isaiah 61:10)*

In Jesus Christ, all things *are* made new!

> *If anyone is in Christ, (she) is a new creature;*
> *the old things passed away; behold, new things have come.*
> *(2 Corinthians 5:17)*

Heart Check

On your own, or preferably with a trusted friend or prayer group, go through the following list and check any ways that shame has been a part of your life. If the sin is in regard to abuse that was inflicted upon you, remember that that part of it is not *your* sin. Your own confession will be based on your *own* sin responses.

- ❏ I feel like I am constantly living with a secret that I am afraid others will find out about.
- ❏ I am unable to form close, trusting friendships and relationships.
- ❏ I live in fear of rejection if this secret is discovered.

- ❏ I do not believe God can ever fully forgive me.
- ❏ I do not believe my friends, husband, parents, church family, etc. can ever understand or forgive my sin.
- ❏ I struggle with inferiority.
- ❏ I have low self-worth/self-image.
- ❏ I suffer condemnation, and from what seem to be voices in my head telling me that I am worthless and will never deserve love, that I will never amount to anything.
- ❏ I cannot forgive myself.
- ❏ I constantly battle tormenting thoughts and memories about my sin, or about the relationships and circumstances surrounding it.
- ❏ I have nightmares.
- ❏ I believe I can never be completely whole or pure again.
- ❏ I do not believe I can ever have a godly husband and/or a healthy, satisfying marriage.

Take these items you've checked before the Lord in prayer. Imagine that you are Photini. Jesus' hand is extended to you in welcome and acceptance. His heart and eyes are warm with compassion. Confess to Him these feelings and thoughts you've checked. Receive His love and forgiveness. Tell the enemy and his tormenting lies to be gone from your thinking and life, in Jesus' name!

Now, without condemnation, let's press on. God wants you free of shame and living in the reality of His abundant love for you! "Therefore there is now no condemnation for those who are in Christ Jesus. For the law of the Spirit of life in Christ Jesus has set you free from the law of sin and of death" (Romans 8:1–2).

Soul Ties as a Result of Sexual Sin

Sex is more than a physical encounter. It is the joining of two persons, and results in lasting bonds that persist on an emotional and spiritual level long after a relationship or encounter has ended. These bonds, sometimes known as "soul ties," can continue to energize things like shame, sorrow, regret, fear, anger, and bitterness. If so, they need to be renounced and severed, in Jesus' name, and the enemy's jurisdiction over them removed.

It really is helpful, as quoted in Stormie's book above, to make a list of every sexual relationship you've ever had and confess each one specifically to the Lord. As Stormie expressed, this may seem embarrassing. But it's important. This would be a good opportunity to confess before the Lord every related sin and circumstance. Perhaps you've had an affair. Or an abortion. These are certainly painful things to confront. And some wounds will take more time to pray through and heal than others. But be assured: wholeness and healing and cleansing ARE going to be yours, if you allow the Lord to restore you in this way, in His love, mercy, patience, and goodness.

If you are feeling led to do this, find some space and quiet time and take each relationship and circumstance before the Lord in prayer. Without any sense of condemnation, honestly confess your own sin in it. Break and renounce any lingering soul tie that may remain between you and any other persons involved. Command the enemy to flee from your thoughts and emotions. Receive God's love and forgiveness—and rejoice!

He does not treat us as our sins deserve
or repay us according to our iniquities.
For as high as the heavens are above the earth,

> *so great is his love for those who fear him;*
> *as far as the east is from the west,*
> *so far has he removed our transgressions from us.*
> *(Psalm 103:10–12)*

It is all too easy to leave ourselves unguarded in practice with regard to sexual purity, even though, in theory, the desire is there. This can happen for a number of reasons, but one in particular relates to how women tend to experience and act out the sin of *lust*. Whereas men tend to be very aware of—and vocal about—this kind of stronghold, women rarely express it as being a problem. Is this because women do not struggle with lust? Not at all. Is it because of shame? Probably. Shannon Ethridge, in her book *Every Woman's Struggle*, comments on this:

> *Another reason women aren't as open about their sexual struggles is because of the humiliation that comes with giving sex in order to get love. Most women don't brag about the number of sexual partners they've had. That's because for a woman the relationship is the prize; the sex was simply the price she had to pay to get the prize. If she paid the price, but still didn't get the prize, there is an incredible amount of humiliation that comes with that. What woman wants to announce to the world her humiliation?*[3]

Also, women are sometimes less likely than men to recognize lust. Lust in men is generally visual and physical. Lust in women, on the other hand, is usually emotional. This is why men, generally speaking, are more vulnerable to pornography. Women, generally speaking, tend to be more vulnerable to things like romance novels and binge-watching steamy Netflix shows—although, as pornography has more and more permeated our culture, women, too, are increasingly reporting struggling with pornography addiction.

When they fantasize, men usually tend to imagine physical encounters. Women, on the other hand, tend to imagine emotional encounters. Very rarely does a woman fall into a sexual affair without having fallen first emotionally. But whether it enters through the gate of the eyes or the gate of the emotions, lust is lust.

Let's all of us take a close, honest look at our hearts, lives, and relationships, and behavior. Don't brush through this too quickly. Allow the Holy Spirit to speak to you about possible blind spots. This list of questions below is (excerpted and slightly adapted) from Shannon Ethridge's book, *Every Woman's Battle*. Honestly answer each question with a yes or no.

1. Is having a man in your life or finding a husband something that dominates your thoughts?
2. If you have a partner in your life, do you compare him to other men (physically, mentally, emotionally, or spiritually)?
3. If married, do you sometimes think of what your life will be like after your husband is dead, wondering who the "next man" in your life could be?
4. Do you have sexual secrets you don't want anyone else to know about?
5. Do you feel like a nobody if you don't have a love interest in your life? Does a romantic relationship give you a sense of identity?
6. Do you seem to attract bad or dysfunctional relationships with men?

7. Do men accuse you of being manipulative or controlling?
8. Do you feel secretly excited or powerful when you sense that a man finds you attractive?
9. Do you have a difficult time responding to your husband's sexual advances because you feel he should meet your needs first?
10. Is remaining emotionally or physically faithful to one person a challenge for you?
11. Do you often choose your attire in the morning based on the men you will encounter that day?
12. Do you find yourself flirting or using sexual innuendos (even if you do not intend to) when conversing with someone you find attractive?
13. Do you resent the fact that your husband wants sex more often than you do?
14. Do you read romance novels (or watch steamy movies on Netflix, etc.) because of the fantasies they evoke within you or because they arouse you sexually?
15. Have you ever used premarital or extramarital relationships to "medicate" your emotional pain?
16. Is there any area of your sexuality that (1) is not known by your husband, (2) is not approved of by your husband, or (3) does not involve your husband?
17. Do you use pornography, either alone or with your husband?
18. Do you fantasize about being intimate with someone other than your husband?
19. Do you have a problem making and maintaining close female friends?
20. Do you experience same-sex attraction or have you been involved in a romantic same-sex relationship?

21. Do your female friendships ever become so emotionally enmeshed that they take away from your emotional bond/intimacy with your husband?
22. Do you converse with strangers online?
23. Have you ever been unable to concentrate on work, school, or the affairs of your household because of thoughts or feelings you are having about someone else?

There is no magic number of yeses and nos that will determine your level of sexual or emotional integrity. However, it is likely that reading through these questions may have awakened you to the fact that your sexual activity, romantic behavior, or emotional attachments might be out of alignment with God's Word, and a hindrance to your spiritual growth or intimacy in your marriage.[4]

Pray through the items that the Holy Spirit highlights as "yes" answers in your heart. Don't be afraid to call a spade a spade. If the Holy Spirit convicts you it, repent of it, rebuke the enemy's influence in your life because of it, and joyfully receive God's forgiveness.

Then some choices will need to be made. Continuing on in a lifestyle of honor and holiness is a lifelong pursuit. It doesn't just include behavior. It involves what we think, what we watch, what we speak, what we wear. These choices need to be made not out of a heart of legalism, though, but rather out of a heart restored and filled with God's Holy Spirit.

Use the 4 Rs to help you in this process:
Repent of any sins (in thought or deed) of sexual impurity, shame, or lust. Remember that God is a compassionate Father

who is mindful that we are but dust, and is quick to forgive (Psalm 103:8–14). We can approach the throne of grace with confidence! (Hebrews 4:16)

Rebuke the enemy, who doesn't want you to know this! In Jesus' name, bring the sins into the light of God's love and forgiveness, and banish the devil's ability to torment you by keeping them in the dark. Tell the enemy out loud to **be gone**! (Jesus did this; we can, too—Matthew 4:10.)

Receive God's gracious and loving forgiveness. Believe His Word that says you are His precious princess, and that He rejoices and sings over you (Psalm 45:10–14; Zephaniah 3:17).

Replace any areas of sexual sin and shame with honor and confidence in God's complete forgiveness and restoration. Ask God to fill you anew with His Holy Spirit and give you the strength and power to live in honor and holiness in thought, word, and deed.

Isaiah 1:18
"Come now, let us reason together," says the Lord. "Though your sins are like scarlet, they shall be as white as snow; though they are red as crimson, they shall be like wool."

Ephesians 5:3
But among you there must not be even a hint of sexual immorality, or of any kind of impurity, or of greed, because these are improper for God's holy people.

As you break out of any patterns of sexual immorality, shame, and/or lust, use these scriptures to reinforce in your own mind who God has designed and destined you to be. Use the truth of God's Word, and the authority you have in Christ, to fight and renounce the lies of the enemy when they come back to torment your thoughts. Do not allow old mental videos, the words of others, and thoughts of worthlessness or guilt to define you. Those are not who you are!

Then, use the space on the next page to record the dialogue you have with God as you pray about the issues you read and prayed about in this chapter. Listen for His words of encouragement, blessing, and affirmation. Remember His promise that there is no condemnation for those who are in Christ (Romans 8:1). Remember that you are His princess!

What is He saying to you about His great love and tender mercy? Record those thoughts here:

Refer back to this when you have doubts or thoughts of condemnation and shame. When we know (and live in) the truth, it sets us free! (John 8:32)

A Circle of Sisters

Use the following questions to jump start your conversation with the Lord—or with your friend(s) if you are doing this in a group. Remember we are all in different places on this journey of restoration, so just do as you feel led. (If you want to talk/pray with someone about these issues (or others), seek out a trusted friend, pastor, mentor, or counselor.)

1. How is the world's (popular culture's) attitude about our sexuality different from what we read in God's Word?

2. What encouraged you in this chapter? What challenged you?

3. Look back to what you wrote down on page 64 as you thought about God's great, over-the-top love for you. You are cherished! How do you think living in this truth can change the way you think/feel/live?

Be open with one another. Confess your areas of weakness to one another. If time and comfort levels permit, use the 4-R prayer model to pray through this area of restoration. Pray *for* one another as well. And remember, **what's prayed in the group, stays in the group!**

Notes and Prayers

_____
_____
_____
_____
_____
_____

CHAPTER SEVEN

secure

*He tends his flock like a shepherd: He gathers the lambs
in his arms and carries them close to his heart;
he gently leads those that have young.
(Isaiah 40:11)*

Sometimes life deals hard blows. Maybe you've seen it. Statistically, you are likely to have experienced it. The truth is, many women have at some point in their lives found themselves in a precarious and devastating position—physically, emotionally, or spiritually abandoned by authority figures in their life who should have been leading and protecting them.

When this is our story, there are a number of ways we can respond. Some of us respond by *withdrawing*. We deal with our fear, insecurity, and rejection by keeping to ourselves, not willing to risk being let down again. Others of us respond by becoming strong. If no one else is going to step up to the plate, we reason, we will take care of ourselves and the people around us. We protect ourselves with assertiveness. Both of these can be described as a self-protective form of independence.

Now, it's not that *independence* (in the good sense) is not good and necessary. But we're not talking about the healthy kind of independence that helps a child learn to tie her shoes, drive a car, and grow into a self-confident member of society. Rather, we're talking about the kinds of "independence" that contribute to isolating us from God and others—expressions of a wounded and insecure heart.

A woman with an insecure heart feels neglected and abandoned. She is distrustful and afraid of being hurt, let down, or abused by those in authority. She often feels solely responsible to take care of herself and/or the people around her. In her mind, parents, step-parents, grandparents, husband(s), and others have failed her. Because of this, she cannot relate properly to people around her, or to her heavenly Father. She may cover her distrust under a façade of meekness, behind a gregarious personality, or with a manner of calm efficiency. But the problem cannot be hidden indefinitely.

God is not like an earthly father. Even the best of dads has his flaws, but God is perfect in every way. He will never let us down, forsake us, abandon us, or abuse us. He will always be there when we need him. He is the ultimate Shepherd, and if we want to be able to connect at a heart level with our heavenly Shepherd, we have to rid ourselves of any warped images we may have of Him due to injustices we suffered at the hands of earthly authorities. These injustices may have been very real; or they may have been only perceived. Either way, the hurt we feel is authentic. But we have to surrender any feelings of rejection, abandonment, or distrust that get in the way of our spiritual, emotional, and relational well-being. That means forgiving any who have hurt us. We can't insulate and protect ourselves with an independent spirit or through isolation.

Heart Check

Take Inventory

Think especially about your relationships with those who have been your primary authorities throughout your life. (Be mindful that we are doing this to gain understanding of ourselves, not to cast blame on them.) Check all that apply:

- ❏ My parents divorced when I was a child, and/or one or the other was never around.
- ❏ My parents had addictions (alcohol, drugs, gambling, etc.).
- ❏ My parents (mother, father, or both) were emotionally distant.
- ❏ My parents (mother, father, or both) worked or traveled extensively, and were often not home.
- ❏ My parents did not give me a great deal of guidance with regard to things like my education, values, goals, or God's destiny for my life.
- ❏ My parents did not practice fair, firm, and consistent discipline with me.
- ❏ My parents were permissive; I was generally allowed to "have my own way."
- ❏ My parents were overly harsh.
- ❏ Our home was frequently chaotic and out of order.
- ❏ One parent did not defend or protect me from the other parent when he or she should have.
- ❏ As a child, I was physically, sexually, verbally, or emotionally abused.
- ❏ I had a lot of sexual relationships before marriage.
- ❏ I have been sexually assaulted.
- ❏ I have a history of broken relationships.

- ❏ I have experienced an abusive relationship(s).
- ❏ I have experienced unethical or immoral leadership in a church.
- ❏ I have been abandoned or significantly let down by my husband (divorce, separation, infidelity, lack of leadership, drugs or alcohol, gambling, apathy, etc.)
- ❏ I feel a heavy, even overwhelming, weight of responsibility for myself and my household.

Look back over your inventory. It's certainly not a given, but the more items you checked, the greater your chances of having an insecure heart. So, then evaluate: if this is the case, how has your insecure heart expressed itself? Which form of self-protection (if any) best describes you?

Inward

- ❏ I am fearful of relationships; I tend to be a loner.
- ❏ I lack confidence in myself.
- ❏ I do not initiate with people, or with new situations.
- ❏ I feel unattractive and/or unintelligent.
- ❏ I want to hide.
- ❏ My life is wrapped up in my children or family. I feel safe with them.
- ❏ I fear other people's rejection or disapproval.
- ❏ I tend to put people in authority on a pedestal.
- ❏ I feel inferior.
- ❏ I am dependent on others.
- ❏ I am overly fearful of others' disapproval (e.g., partner, parents, employers, teachers, authorities, etc.)

Outward

- ❏ I have a lot of friends (some might say too many), but few close ones.
- ❏ I come off as extremely self-confident.
- ❏ I thrive on new relationships and situations.
- ❏ I try to think the best of myself.
- ❏ I tend to show off.
- ❏ I sometimes go so fast/get so busy that I leave my friends/family in my dust.
- ❏ I don't really care about what others think (or I act like I don't).
- ❏ I try to bring people in authority down to my level.
- ❏ I tend to feel superior.
- ❏ I don't need anyone else.
- ❏ I am not afraid to risk others' disapproval (e.g., partner, parents, employers, teachers, authorities, etc.)

The woman who expresses her insecurity through outward self-protection (assertiveness, striving) has the same feelings, deep down, as the woman who expresses hers through inward self-protection (withdrawal, isolation). Both are rooted in fear and rejection. Both directly contradict what God says about Himself, us, and His love and care for us. Both are forms of self-reliance and (the wrong kind of) independence. An insecure heart builds a fortress around itself that seeks to protect itself first and foremost.

Healing for the Independent Heart

There are three irreducible components to the healing of an independent heart. The first is **repentance**. The second is **humility**.

The third is **faith**. Look for all three of these components in David's heartfelt prayer in Psalm 5:

> *Have mercy on me, O God, according to your unfailing love; according to your great compassion; blot out my transgressions. Wash away all my iniquity and cleanse me from my sin. For I know my transgressions, and my sin is always before me. Against you, you only, have I sinned and done what is evil in your sight, so that you are proved right when you speak and justified when you judge. . . . Hide your face from my sins and blot out all my iniquity. Create in me a pure heart, O God, and renew a steadfast spirit within me. Do not cast me from your presence or take your Holy Spirit from me. Restore to me the joy of your salvation and grant me a willing spirit, to sustain me. (Psalm 51:1–4, 9–12)*

See if you can find in the passage above:

Phrases that refer to repentance:

_____

_____

Phrases that refer to humility:

_____

_____

Phrases that refer to faith:

_____

_____

Consider the characteristics, mentioned above, of an insecure heart. Ask the Holy Spirit to show you any ways you may be operating in this heart condition. It's not easy to admit that these things may be part of our personality. But even though we may have a sincere love for God, some of these things may still be evident in our life. Please be open to this thought and willing to self-examine yourself. We can't be truly repentant unless, first, we are truly honest. Then:

Repent of every characteristic and expression of an insecure and independent heart that is evident in your personality or your actions.

Rebuke any influence the enemy of your soul may have in or through your life because of them. Renounce the comfort and protection you have received from them.

Replace them with the comfort of God's Holy Spirit, the truth of His Word, and the protection of His authority.

Receive God's forgiveness. Accept no thoughts of condemnation, sorrow, or regret. This is a new day!

> *Therefore, there is now no condemnation*
> *for those who are in Christ Jesus,*
> *because through Christ Jesus the law of the Spirit*
> *of life set me free*
> *from the law of sin and death.*
> *(Romans 8:1–2)*

In the space provided on the next page, identify and write down the opposite attitude or behavior of what you repented of (for example, instead of "critical," you might write "patient"). Commit yourself to "putting off the old, and putting on the new." These new attitudes and behaviors are part of who you *really* are, in Christ!

> *You were taught, with regard to your former way of life,*
> *to put off your old self,*
> *which is being corrupted by its deceitful desires;*
> *to be made new in the attitude of your minds;*
> *and to put on the new self, created to be like God*
> *in true righteousness and holiness. (Ephesians 4:22–24)*

SECURE

Old Attitude/Behavior   New Attitude/Behavior

Then, put your own name in the blanks below and pray through Ephesians 3:16–19:

"Dear God, I, _____, pray that out of (Your) glorious riches (You will) strengthen (me), _____, with power through (Your) Spirit in (my) inner being, so that Christ may dwell in (my) heart through faith. And I, _____, pray that I, _____, being rooted and established in love, may have power, together with all the saints, to grasp how wide and long and high and deep is the love of Christ, and to know this love that surpasses knowledge—that I, _____, may be filled to the measure of all the fullness of God."

There IS healing for a wounded, insecure, and independent heart, but it requires a heartfelt commitment to repentance, humility, and faith. It comes as we begin to experience and live in the truth of how much God loves us. It comes as we develop a personality that is centered around serving and trusting Him, instead of protecting and defending ourselves. And it comes as we learn to live in security and dependence—not on our own coping mechanisms, or on substitute shepherds—but on our *true* Shepherd, the Lord Jesus Christ.

*For you were like sheep going astray,
but now you have returned
to the Shepherd and Overseer of your souls.*
(1 Peter 2:25)

A Circle of Sisters

1. In what ways is independence a good thing? In what ways can we take it to an extreme when we want to protect ourselves? How do you see this playing out in your own life?

2. Do you see the relationships between insecurity and independence? How does (the wrong kind of) independence affect relationships? (Think of friendships, marriages, parent/child, employee/employer relationships, unity in the Body of Christ, etc.)

3. Look back at the scriptures you read in this chapter, and think about others that have been highlighted in this study. What scriptures or thoughts have stood out to you most? Why?

4. If God is leading you in the area of healing and restoration for insecurity, what do you sense Him saying to you? If you are meeting with a friend or a group, share your thoughts with one another, and pray for each other.

Notes and Prayers

CHAPTER EIGHT
Faithful

The Lord is faithful to all His promises and loving toward all He has made.
Psalm 145: 13b

Jesus demonstrated in His story about the maidens and the bridegroom (see Matthew 25) that "ready" hearts are *faithful* hearts—watchful and prepared, steady and focused, excited and expectant. But in this story He also revealed something else. He communicated something about Himself so exciting it should immediately grip our emotions and imaginations—something that should keep us fervent, focused, and ready to be faithful at all costs!

When we think of the word "faithful" in the context of marriage, it takes on an even more intense and intimate quality. When a bride makes a vow of faithfulness to her husband on their wedding day, she is not thinking about duty or obligation. Her vows are inspired by passion, affection, and a burning desire to please her beloved. In the same way, her bridegroom's vows to her are based on his desire to cherish, protect, and provide for her all the days of their life together. Their covenant of marriage is based on love and great joy. This is Jesus' heart for His Church—and for *you*.

God doesn't want to have a relationship with you based on duty. He wants a relationship based on love!

> *"In that day," declares the Lord,*
> *"you will call me 'my husband';*
> *you will no longer call me 'my master.'"*
> *(Hosea 2:16)*

The five unfaithful women in Jesus' story were waiting out of *duty*.
The five faithful ones were waiting out of *love*.

The ten women who waited for the Bridegroom knew for whom they were waiting. They were all fully aware of the promise of celebration when He arrived. Yet when it came right down to it, only five actually entered into the festivities. Obviously, there were fundamental differences between the ones who were ready, and the ones who were not.

What caused the five to let their lamps run dry? Why weren't they ready? Why were they unfaithful—and what can we learn from their mistakes? Let's examine our own hearts. Let's take a look at what might cause *us* to run out of "oil"—to be found unprepared, unfaithful, and unfulfilled in our own relationship with the Bridegroom.

The Faithful Heart

The most obvious reason the five foolish women missed out on the celebration is that they allowed their lamps to run low on oil. While they were gone to find more, the Bridegroom arrived. "Ready or not . . ."—and they were not! The other five were able to remain faithful because they kept their lamps full of oil. They entered into the festivities while the five with no oil watched from the sidelines.

Sometimes we, too, find our lamps going dry. The Oil Supply slows to a trickle and we can't seem to get it going again. So we wander off on our own to find some oil. We are no longer faithfully attending our Bridegroom—although we may deceive ourselves that we are. Yet we find ourselves watching from the sidelines—peeking through the window watching others enjoy rich fellowship with the Lord, while we seem to be missing out.

What's going on? What has stopped the oil of God's Holy Spirit from flowing freely in our hearts and lives? Most importantly, how can we start it up again—without going off to look for it elsewhere?

Heart Check

If you were among the group of ten women waiting for the bridegroom, in which half would you find yourself? Would you be among the five who were faithful and ready? Or might you be among the five who were not? Take a good, hard, honest look at your life, and your own relationship with the Bridegroom. Have you been distracted? Have you run out of oil? Has the enemy succeeded in preventing you from receiving all that Jesus has secured for you? Think about what Jesus came to bring us, from Luke 4:18–19. In this passage, which many have called His "mission statement," Jesus said He came to bring Good News, freedom, healing, and favor. Check your own heart for where you stand on each one:

1. Good News

Have I personally received the Good News of the gospel—reconciled to God by faith in Jesus Christ? Am I growing in joyful intimacy with the Bridegroom? Is my relationship with Him a source of good news for others?

2. Freedom

What are the strongholds that have kept me in emotional and spiritual captivity? Have I truly *repented* of them, *rebuked* the enemy's influence in my life through them, *replaced* them with truth and obedience, and *received* God's forgiveness and the filling of His Holy Spirit to live differently? Am I living free of the enemy's schemes to distract, deceive, and enslave me?

3. Healing

Are there any unhealed wounds from the past that are still open sores in my spirit? Do I experience illnesses and infirmities that may be physical manifestations of spiritual or emotional issues? Have I sought the Lord for healing in *every* area of my life?

4. Favor

Am I one of the five women who were able to celebrate freely with the Bridegroom? Or am I one who is watching from the sidelines?

Check your "spiritual oil supply." How would you rate it?

0	1	2	3	4	5	6	7	8	9	10
Empty		Low		Half-full		Moderate			Overflowing!	

**Let's make sure the oil of God's Holy Spirit
is flowing clean, clear,
and abundantly in our hearts!**

Imagine each unrepentant sin of thought, emotion, action, or omission as a brick in the construction of a stronghold. After a while, those bricks pile up, and the release of God's Holy Spirit into our life is effectually blocked—cutting off our Oil Supply. The stronghold is established in our heart, where it filters our view of God and other people and influences our thoughts, emotions, and actions. We justify it as a part of our personality, our upbringing, or our worldview—and the enemy's scheme is set into motion.

*". . . in order that Satan might not outwit us.
For we are not unaware of his schemes."
(2 Corinthians 2:11)*

Beware of the Wrong Oil

When we put oil in any kind of machinery, we need to make sure it's the right kind of oil. We wouldn't put kerosene in a car engine, nor would we put motor oil in a kerosene heater. The same is true of our spiritual oil tanks!

The typical response to a wound or area of insecurity is to try to deal with it ourselves—to comfort, protect, and provide for the area of woundedness, weakness, or fear. This is the scheme of the enemy: to sell us the wrong oil! In the story of the ten maidens, the women who ran out of oil were distracted by running into town to try to buy more. (Matthew 25:9) Jesus, on the other hand said, "Come to *me*, all you who are weary and burdened, and *I* will give you rest. (Matthew 11:28, emphasis added)

When we are hurt or fearful, we can tend to rely on our natural, self-defensive coping mechanisms, instead of turning to the Lord to comfort and defend us. We may as well call these coping mechanisms "false comforts." But false comforts are the wrong oil for our lamps!

Unfortunately, God's people through the ages have learned this lesson the hard way. Take some time to read 1 Corinthians 10:1–14, where the apostle Paul reminds us what happened to the Israelites when they wandered in the desert, in limbo between Egypt and the Promised Land. Notice what happened when they turned to "false comforts." And notice the Biblical term for false comforts: *idolatry.*

One would think that after such a miraculous and dramatic delivery from captivity in Egypt, the Israelites' hearts would immediately be faithful to their Deliverer. Yet the wilderness experience, as it tested their hearts, revealed gross unbelief and idolatry. In their impatience while waiting for Moses to come back down the mountain with the Ten Commandments, the Israelites created a golden calf as an object of worship, in order to alleviate their anxiety (see Exodus 32:1–4).

Idolatry was lurking in their hearts, and having to wait on God exposed it.

Heart Check

The Israelites turned to an idol instead of waiting for Moses to arrive. The ten bridesmaids in Jesus' story ran off to buy oil instead of waiting for the Bridegroom. Take a look at your own life. Does idolatry lurk in *your* heart? When God seems to withhold His presence or provision, to what—or to whom—do you run?

There are many idols, or "false comforts," to which we can turn in our attempt to secure, comfort, or numb ourselves when God seems far away or slow to act, such as (but not limited to) the following. Check all those that apply to you (to the extent that you may use them as "false comforts"). *(Note: Many of these are good things in and of themselves; it's when we use them as false comforts in the place of God's presence and provision that they can become "idols.")*

- food
- alcohol, drugs (even prescription)
- shopping
- exercise
- sensuality
- clothing, appearance
- daydreaming, fantasies
- flirtation, immorality
- friends and family
- husband, boyfriend
- children
- house
- entertainment, books
- romance novels, soap operas, Netflix, etc.
- career
- recreation
- volunteering
- church ministry, religious activities
- activities, clubs, hobbies
- education
- busy-ness
- striving, ambition, achievement
- self-pity
- victimization, martyrdom
- control
- worry
- bitterness, grudge-holding
- pride
- astrology, mysticism
- any occult involvement

If you checked any of these as "false comforts" for you, you can use the 4-R prayer outline to guide you as you confess them to the Lord. In faith, receive the true comfort of His Spirit, His presence, His protection, and His provision. Ask Him to show you what that faith will look like, practically speaking. Write it out below:

Faith is believing God—that He is who He says He is, that He will do what He says He will do, and that I am who He says I am. When hurts, insecurities, fears, and difficulties arise, we mustn't succumb to a knee-jerk reaction to resort to the old false comforts. We need to learn to look with *spiritual* eyes: *What is the enemy's scheme? What false comfort am I tempted to seek?* Remember:

1. False comforts are coping mechanisms that are not of God's Holy Spirit, that help us manage stronghold issues.

2. False comforts can be material, emotional, physical, or spiritual.

3. False comforts are idolatry—relying on something else to comfort and secure ourselves instead of turning to and trusting in God.

The Spirit-filled life of faithfulness to the Bridegroom is all about love, not duty. It's relationship, not religion. Instead of living to gratify the impulses of our emotions and cravings, instead of being influenced and trapped by the snares of our enemy, the devil, we can live freely, joyfully, and faithfully in Christ. The work has already been done. The provision has been made. The freedom has been won. Walking in it is up to us!

Following are some biblical truths that expand on what we've already learned about having a faithful heart. Use them as replacement attitudes and actions as you tear down strongholds of wrong thinking and false comforts—replacing them instead with a righteous stronghold of grateful, joyful, and passionate faithfulness to your Bridegroom, overflowing with the oil of His Spirit!

- ❏ I will see myself as God sees me—pure and unblemished, cherished and enjoyed—like a bride robed in Jesus' own righteousness. (Isaiah 61:10)
- ❏ I will not turn to false comforts to cope with my unhealed wounds, insecurities, or fears.
- ❏ I will receive God's comfort for all those, trusting Him to protect, provide, comfort, and avenge.
- ❏ I will not accept the lie that *"I am the way I am, and I will never change."*
- ❏ I will honestly and humbly recognize attitudes and behaviors in my life that are false comforts, and I will confront their root issues with truth, obedience, and faith.
- ❏ I will be faithful to Jesus Christ out of a love relationship, not out of religious duty.
- ❏ I will not isolate myself or go off "on my own" to deal with my problems.
- ❏ I will live mindful of how much Jesus Christ has forgiven me, and I will extend that forgiveness, mercy, and grace to others.
- ❏ I will remember God's faithfulness to me in any and all circumstances—even despite my own faithlessness. (2 Timothy 2:13; 2 Thessalonians 3:3)

- ❏ When my joy seems dim, I will come to Him for the "oil" I need—in His Word, prayer, worship, fellowship with other believers, etc.
- ❏ I will make my relationship with my Bridegroom the number one joy and priority of my life.

Galatians 5:22–25
*But the fruit of the Spirit is love, joy, peace, patience, kindness, goodness, **faithfulness**, gentleness and self-control. Against such things there is no law. Those who belong to Christ Jesus have crucified the sinful nature with its passions and desires. Since we live by the Spirit, let us keep in step with the Spirit.*

A Circle of Sisters

1. Consider the list above and choose one or two that especially speak to you and where you are in your walk with the Lord right now. Write them below and share them with the group.

2. How does our culture encourage the use of "false comforts"?

FAITHFUL

How does it promote "idolatry"?

3. What will it really look like to step out in faith, refuse distractions and false comforts, and serve/love God wholeheartedly?

The answers will be different for each of us. You can encourage one another by sharing creative ideas for walking in faithfulness, with ready hearts, like the women in Jesus' parable.

"Let us examine our ways and test them,
and let us return to the Lord.
Let us lift up our hearts and our hands to God in heaven . . ."
(Lamentations 3:40–42)

If you are doing this with a friend or a group, share your thoughts with one another and encourage one another in walking out your declarations. Spend some time praying for one another, specifically related to each woman's unique journey.

Notes and Prayers

CHAPTER NINE
a Blessing

But no one can tame the tongue . . .
with it we bless our Lord and Father,
and with it we curse men, who have been made
in the likeness of God;
from the same mouth come both blessing and cursing.
My (sisters), these things ought not to be this way.
James 3:9–10

Think about walking into a home where fresh bread is just coming out of the oven. Mmmm . . . so warm and inviting! Then think about walking into a pig barn (or being anywhere near a pig barn) . . . eeew! We want to stay as far away as possible! Sometimes, there can even be a malignant quality in the air that we can't perceive with our natural senses. Unseen poisonous gases, when undetected, have been known to cause sickness and even death.

How about when people enter your home, your office, or wherever you spend a lot of time? What kind of "aroma" is in the air? Not the smell—the *feeling*. Is it warm and inviting? Is it "blessing and grace"?

The free release of blessing, by words and actions, is a powerful tool that changes the spiritual atmosphere around us. The apostle Paul wrote, "But thanks be to God, who always leads us in triumphal procession in Christ and through us spreads everywhere the fragrance of the knowledge of him. For we are to God the aroma of Christ among those who are being saved and those who are perishing" (2 Corinthians 2:14–15). When we live in a constant attitude and practice of blessing toward others, we are essentially creating and maintaining an atmosphere that is hostile to Satan. We are resisting him, so he must flee! (James 4:7)

Can you easily speak words of encouragement, destiny, grace, and hope to your children? Your friends or husband? Neighbors, extended family, and co-workers? Others around you? As followers of Jesus and filled with His Spirit, we can be women who freely bless; anything less falls short of God's divine intention. Blessing should be liberally and generously flowing out of us like a fountain of fragrant, sweet-smelling oil!

Reality check! What is coming out of our mouths and attitudes? Let's confess and repent of withholding blessing (and even outright "cursing" sometimes), and replace it with the grace of freely blessing others. May we be known as women of blessing, and may other people long to be around us—because God's blessing, favor, and grace are constantly and freely released from within us!

No Withholding

God designed our tongues to be fountains of blessing, releasing His love, power, healing, and grace on the people around us.

A BLESSING

When we freely bless, we release words of God's favor upon people like a spring of water bubbling out fresh water (James 3:11).

When we *withhold blessing*, on the other hand, we hold back this refreshment from the people God has placed in our lives. This is also true when we *"curse"*; that is, when we release words that insult, offend, accuse, or blame. Whether we curse or simply deny blessing where blessing is due, we hold back from people the demonstration of God's love and grace, and can even open up a spiritual advantage and opportunity to the devil.

Withholding blessing goes against the essential nature of our purpose, for every follower of Jesus is a "priest": "But you are a chosen people, *a royal priesthood*, a holy nation, a people belonging to God, that you may declare the praises of him who called you out of darkness into his wonderful light" (1 Peter 2:9). As we freely speak and pray blessing over people, God does bless. Words that edify, encourage, and strengthen are empowered by God, and used to pour out His blessing upon people when we invoke His name on them.

However, when we withhold blessing (or we "curse"), it:

- causes discouragement, rejection, and offense
- creates opportunities for the enemy to deceive and influence people through perceived rejection, hurt feelings, condemnation, self-hatred, and bitterness
- dampens people's desire to please and serve
- blocks the release of God's favor
- robs joy from us and from others
- creates an atmosphere that is spiritually and emotionally cold
- compromises our role as "priests"

- ensures God's word is not communicated with blessing, and His people are not ministered to with grace
- causes us to misrepresent God (this is the sin for which Moses was denied entrance to the Promised Land!)
- denies our children (and others around us), the security and affirmation that they need to grow emotionally strong and healthy
- robs our families of generational blessings

In your Bible, read the story of King Saul, Jonathan, and David in 1 Samuel, chapters 18 to 20. Trace and note the results of Saul's sin of "withholding blessing" from David. Jot these down below:

Then read 2 Samuel 9. What a beautiful story of blessing! What are your observations about how David responded to Saul's family, despite how Saul had treated him?

Heart Check

Are you a blesser? Or do you withhold blessing? As you consider the following characteristics of withholding blessing, evaluate to what extent these statements describe you:

❏ I am reticent to thank and complement others.
❏ I feel responsible to correct others' shortcomings and uphold high standards for them.
❏ I find it difficult to freely rejoice in others' successes.
❏ I cannot be kind and gracious to those whom I feel do not "deserve" it.
❏ I retaliate when hurt or offended.
❏ I sometimes lose my cool and unleash a torrent of angry words on the people around me.
❏ I give others the "cold shoulder," or the "silent treatment," when I am angry.
❏ I tend to be sarcastic, sometimes passing it off as humor.
❏ I am uncomfortable expressing sympathy and compassion.
❏ I am uncomfortable expressing my emotions.
❏ I do not like to show or receive physical demonstrations of affection (hugs, etc.)
❏ People find me uncommunicative, intimidating, and/or difficult to please.
❏ I don't like to talk to people whom I don't know well.
❏ I am uncomfortable praying in public.
❏ I rarely expend the time or emotional energy to uplift and encourage the people around me, either in word or in deed.
❏ I am more comfortable sharing from my head (information) than from my heart (affirmation).
❏ I am uncomfortable saying, "I love you."

Repent of the sin (name it specifically, and what it looks like in your own life, words, actions, and attitudes).

Rebuke the enemy and his influence in and through your life because of it.

Replace the sin by affirming the truth and walking continuously in the opposite spirit. Memorize and meditate on what is true (use Scripture; you can start with the ones below).

Receive God's forgiveness, and the empowering of His Holy Spirit to live in the truth.

Read and think about the following scriptures:

Proverbs 25:11
"A word aptly spoken is like apples of gold in settings of silver."

Proverbs 27:9
"Perfume and incense bring joy to the heart, and the pleasantness of one's friend springs from his earnest counsel."

Matthew 12:34b–36
"For out of the overflow of the heart the mouth speaks. The good man brings good things out of the good stored up in him, and the evil man brings evil things out of the evil stored up in him. But I tell you that men will have to give account on the day of judgment for every careless word they have spoken."

Romans 12:14
"Bless those who persecute you; bless and do not curse."

1 Corinthians 4:12–13a
"When we are cursed, we bless; when we are persecuted, we endure it; when we are slandered, we answer kindly."

1 Peter 3:9
"Do not repay evil with evil or insult with insult, but with blessing, because to this you were called so that you may inherit a blessing."

A Circle of Sisters

1. How does the environment you were raised in affect your ability to bless others—either verbally or with your actions (or both)?

2. After this chapter on blessing versus withholding, in what ways do you sense God leading you to repent and make changes?

3. What scriptures above encourage and inspire you in this?

Make the following declarations aloud, either on your own or with any friends you are meeting with:

- ❏ I will freely, generously, and sincerely thank and complement others, especially those closest to me.
- ❏ I will not withhold blessing from others because of my own feelings of inadequacy.
- ❏ I will rejoice at and "cheerlead" the efforts and successes of people around me.
- ❏ I will speak kindly and graciously, even to those whom I do not feel "deserve" it.
- ❏ I will bless those who insult and persecute me.
- ❏ I will willingly and eagerly pray for others, both privately and publicly.
- ❏ When I pray for others, privately or publicly, I will pray prayers of blessing that invoke God's name and favor over their lives.
- ❏ I will speak with sincerity, and will not use sarcasm or derogatory comments to cover anger, resentment, or dissatisfaction with others.
- ❏ I will make an effort to speak to, and get to know, people who are new to me.

A BLESSING

- ❏ I will expend the time and emotional energy to encourage and uplift the people around me.
- ❏ I will minister to others from my heart (affirmation), not just from my head (information).
- ❏ I will speak words of love, destiny, and blessing to my family and friends on a regular basis.

Afterwards, take this opportunity to speak and/or pray blessing over one another. See how you can send your friends and family out the door with a word of encouragement every day!

Notes and Prayers

_____
_____
_____
_____
_____
_____
_____
_____
_____
_____

ENCOUNTERS AT THE WELL

Notes and Prayers

ENDNOTES

1. The 4 Rs are adapted from the *Living Set Free in Christ Course Manual*, by Mike Riches, © 2011 SycPub Global, Gig Harbor, WA. Used by permission.
2. Omartian, Stormie, *Lord, I Want to Be Whole*, Thomas Nelson Publishers: Nashville, TN, 2000, p. 43
3. Ethridge, Shannon, *Every Woman's Battle*, Waterbrook Press, Colorado Springs, CO: 2003, p. 45.
4. *Every Woman's Battle*, p. 15–17

ACKNOWLEDGMENTS

To my husband, Doug: thank you for always encouraging me in my gifts and pursuits, and for your patience with all the rabbit trails I often take along the way! Your love and faithfulness to me, the Lord, and our family have provided a shelter that serves as both a solid rock and a safe place to land for all of us. Not to mention, you make things a lot more fun, adventurous, and well-organized along the way! I could not do life and ministry without you.

To Mike Riches, my pastor of over thirty years: you and Cindy have been the "tip of the spear" in bringing the Living Set Free truths to not only our church family but to the Body of Christ at large and to the nations. Your contributions to this book and my own life are immeasurable.

To the friends, mentors, and church leaders with whom I've been privileged to serve the Lord, I thank God for you every day. This book—and many of my own "encounters at the well" with Jesus—happened because of your influence in my life.

To my team at Inspira, it is a joy to make beautiful books with you all. You will not likely realize the massive impact of your work till you get to Heaven. Your gifts and talents make it possible for so many authors to bring their God-given messages and missions to the world.

ABOUT THE AUTHOR

Arlyn Lawrence finds great joy in making God's Word relevant to everyday life and living, and in helping people of all ages find hope and transformation through Jesus Christ. She is passionate about prayer and its role in helping Jesus-followers experience the presence and power of God in their lives.

Arlyn has been the editor, author, or co-author of numerous books and curricular resources published and distributed around the world, including *Prayer-Saturated Kids* (Tyndale), *PrayKids! A Hands-On Guide for Developing Kids Who Pray* (NavPress), *Living Set Free in Christ* (SycPub Global), and the *What I Wish I Knew at 18 Leadership and Lifeskills Curriculum* for teens and *Parenting for the Launch: Raising Teens to Succeed in the Real World* (LifeSmart). She also served as an editor for *Pray!* magazine (Navpress) and was the author of one of its regular columns, "Intercession Ignited." Through the company she started in 2014, Inspira Literary Solutions, Arlyn has helped many dozens of authors bring their own books to publication (www.inspiralit.com).

Arlyn lives on an island in the Puget Sound in beautiful Washington State with her husband, Doug, their dog, and numerous chickens, enjoying the frequent company of their five adult children and spouses and a growing brood of delightful grandchildren.

You can reach Arlyn at info@inspiralit.com.

www.ingramcontent.com/pod-product-compliance
Lightning Source LLC
Chambersburg PA
CBHW070116080526
44586CB00013B/1310